More Memories
of
Northampton

The publishers would like to thank the following companies for their support in the production of this book

A Bell & Co

C Butt

The Brixworth Engineering Company Ltd

Crane Hill Engineering

Cosworth Racing

Crockett & Jones

Dennis Faulkner & Alsop

Dove Naish

E&A Plant

Peter Haddon & Partners

Howard Associates

Merrys

Moulton School

Moulton College

Pianoforte Supplies Ltd

Quinton House School

Westbridge Motors

S E Wilkinson & Son

First published in Great Britain by True North Books Limited
England HX5 9AE
01422 377977

ISBN 1 903204 34 8
Text, design and origination by True North Books Limited
Printed and bound by The Amadeus Press Limited

More Memories
of
Northampton

Edited by Alan Burman

Contents

Northampton through the ages

Welcome to 'More Memories of Northampton', a new collection of nostalgic images from the last century. Accompanied by informative and thought provoking text, the photographs will take you on a magical mystery tour that the Beatles sang about in the swinging 60s. The book is not meant to be a historical tome full of dry facts, but one that will fire the imagination and awaken memories of days through which you and your immediate ancestors lived. 'More Memories of Northampton' will bring flooding back the days when there was more to life in the town than a visit to the Grosvenor Centre. Relive an era when we passed shillings and half crowns ' across the counter. Go back to an age when market traders were not prosecuted for weighing bananas by the pound.

As you do, recall what it was in our town's history that made Northampton a grand place in which to be brought up. It has a fine historic tradition. There is evidence of activity in the Iron Age and in Roman times. Then there came Saxon settlements in the middle of the seventh century. Northampton soon became one of the most important towns in Mercia. The warlike Danes swept across the area in the ninth century, making it their administrative centre, to be followed by the Normans after the conquest of 1066. The impressive and imposing Northampton Castle made the town even more important to the region's stability. In the Domesday Book it was described as being a place of 300 houses, yielding a levy of £30. By the early 12th century that had trebled, illustrating that Northampton had become a wealthy and successful part of the country. The granting of a charter in 1189 rewarded its financial support for Richard the Lionheart's crusades. His brother, King John, confirmed this in 1200. Northampton now had the right to have a mayor.

Not everything was sweetness and light. In 1164

Henry II had Thomas a Becket, the Archbishop of Canterbury, put on trial here. That 'turbulent priest', as the King described him, escaped to France, but was killed by Henry's agents in 1170 on the steps of Canterbury Cathedral. In the Middle Ages, financial problems and the effects of the plague hit Northampton. Many great buildings were destroyed in the 17th century Civil War and a great fire in 1675 consumed many of the wooden framed structures. But, the townspeople were made of stern stuff. Already known for its shoe industry, the Industrial Revolution promoted the town's fame. It developed an international reputation as mechanisation of production grew. The coming of the railway age opened up new markets and the population increased tenfold in the 19th century. So well known was the town for its major industry that even the soccer team became known as the 'Cobblers'.

But, it is to the 20th century that we turn for the main thrust of this book. The photographs will make the reader once again recall times when

Newland was an area of interesting architectural styles, with a variety of businesses and little shops that had their own distinctive quality. That was in the days when individuality was important. In many of our nation's towns the shopping centres and High Street giants could be moved from town to town without anyone knowing the difference. 'More Memories of Northampton' will enable the reader to visit the Emporium Arcade once more. You can call in for a pint at The Peacock, that old coaching inn. Entertainment lovers may want to tread the boards that once supported local talent like Des O'Connor and Jim Dale, before they went off to national stardom. It is all here in this latest of the delightful series of books dedicated to allowing readers to wallow in nostalgia.

Whilst technological trends have made life easier for us, it is important not to forget what went before. Then we can appreciate all the better what we have now. We can look back on the days of the dolly tub and donkey stoning the front step with a wry smile. In those days women were proud to be housewives.

Today they apologise for being so. What the modern Ms might learn through turning these pages is that her grandmother had a control over her family by organising the house and taking charge of the finances. Hubby tipped up his wage packet and was given his spends. If a few pints of Phipps and a couple of packets of Players' Weights exhausted his pocket money, then hard luck. He had to wait until the next payday before the missus gave him another allowance. Heaven help him if that pay packet was not handed over unopened! A glimpse at the following pages might make some realise that equality for some women meant an improvement in their husbands' lot. Come back in time as you leaf through the book and remember what was important to us over the last century. Pleasures were simpler and happiness more easily achieved. Just a glimpse of a film star was an occasion. The sound of Johnny 'Cry-baby' Ray coming from a wind up gramophone, the smell of crusty bread from the bakery and the sadness of that last tram ride are memories that will be rekindled in these pages. There are some other things that are painful to remember. The depression days in between the wars, the poor housing conditions in The Boroughs and the bombs that fell on Duston and St Andrew's Hospital should help us be determined never to return to those times. Seeing them again makes us realise how far we have come. But, this book is meant to be more of a celebration and a trip down memory lane than an exercise in social conscience. Let us rejoice about the good times and the fun we had. Take a pleasure in seeing once again what we can of life before the developers moved in. Thanks to the art of the photographer and the powerful tool of our own minds we can enjoy what has been preserved for us from the 20th century. It should help us make sure that everywhere we go today a camera is never far from our side. The next generations deserve to know how we lived and were entertained in the 21st century.

It is time to turn that first page. Get in the right mood by making a cup of Ovaltine. Turn on the wireless and tune it in to the Light Programme or Radio Luxembourg. Suck on a bullseye and tap the ash off a Kensitas cigarette. Go even further back in time and get completely in the nostalgic mood by finding a little cloche hat and flapper dress to wear. Alternatively, put on a smoking jacket and spats. Allow yourself a little violence and smash all the CDs you can find of boy bands and rap artists, rip up the training shoes and be as politically incorrect as you want. The late Ronnie Hilton is singing 'No other love', the Cobblers are at home to Arsenal and Errol Flynn is swashbuckling at the cinema. Beer is a tanner a pint and petrol two bob a gallon. What are you waiting for? It is time to meet the last century head on.

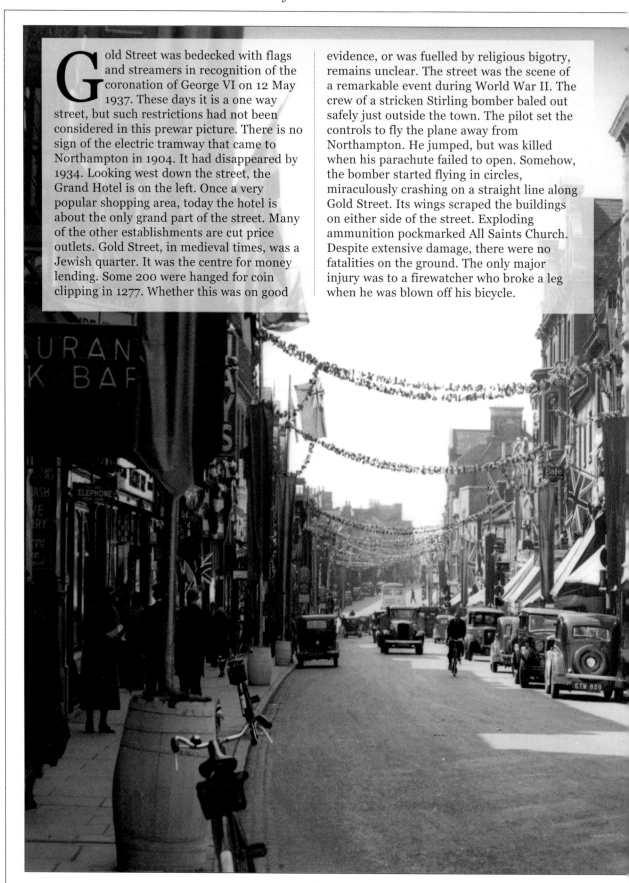

Gold Street was bedecked with flags and streamers in recognition of the coronation of George VI on 12 May 1937. These days it is a one way street, but such restrictions had not been considered in this prewar picture. There is no sign of the electric tramway that came to Northampton in 1904. It had disappeared by 1934. Looking west down the street, the Grand Hotel is on the left. Once a very popular shopping area, today the hotel is about the only grand part of the street. Many of the other establishments are cut price outlets. Gold Street, in medieval times, was a Jewish quarter. It was the centre for money lending. Some 200 were hanged for coin clipping in 1277. Whether this was on good evidence, or was fuelled by religious bigotry, remains unclear. The street was the scene of a remarkable event during World War II. The crew of a stricken Stirling bomber baled out safely just outside the town. The pilot set the controls to fly the plane away from Northampton. He jumped, but was killed when his parachute failed to open. Somehow, the bomber started flying in circles, miraculously crashing on a straight line along Gold Street. Its wings scraped the buildings on either side of the street. Exploding ammunition pockmarked All Saints Church. Despite extensive damage, there were no fatalities on the ground. The only major injury was to a firewatcher who broke a leg when he was blown off his bicycle.

Street Scenes

Below: The day dawned bright and sunny for the coronation of King George VI. His daughter was not to have similar weather 16 years later. Hers was held in damp conditions. It was not the weather that was important. For the British the occasion was everything. In 1937 it was especially significant. The country had undergone the turmoil of the abdication crisis. King George's elder brother had refused to end his relationship with the American socialite Wallis Simpson. In 1936, 'the year of three kings', he became Edward VIII, but had given up the throne by the end of the year. George VI succeeded him with some anxiety, as this was a role for which he was not prepared. The nation rallied to his support. People were determined to show their support for the monarchy. This scene, looking north along the Drapery from All Saints Church, was repeated up and down the land. The Drapery is the name given to this entire street. To be accurate it should only apply to the left hand side. The opposite side is the Glovery, but the term is no longer in use. The names illustrate the trades that flourished here in earlier times. Mercers' Row is to the right of the imposing Westminster Bank building. Philadelphus Jeyes' pharmacy is one of the shops on the west side of the Drapery. It is the name behind Jeyes Fluid. Philadelphus was the town mayor in 1852. The family went in for memorable Christian names. Theophilus Jeyes was the town clerk earlier in the 19th century.

FREEMAN
ARDY & WILLIS
OOTWEAR SPECIALISTS

Right: This was Gas Street, looking into Horseshoe Street, as it was half a century ago. Augustin Street was to the right. The construction of a huge traffic island has completely altered the area. Before the change the Gasometer advertised the local brew, across the road from the Dunlop hoarding. Pubs in those days were often smoky, poorly lit premises. They were designed for drinking, rather than yuppie style comfort. The public bar was often a male preserve. Heaven help a woman, other than the Sally Army girl with the 'War Cry', who invaded this territory. Keen games of bones, fives and threes, don and cribbage were fiercely contested. Cries of 'one for his nob', 'Morgan's orchard', 'four for game' and 'I'm knocking' were like a foreign language to the uninitiated. Yet, when the games were finished, the loser paid his corner and the winner went off into the night. There was no fear of a bunch of lager louts waiting round the corner. Nor was there any chance of being deafened by the trill of mobile phones. More upmarket pubs had lounge bars where a man could take his wife. There were waiters who took the drinks order and deftly carried trays full of glasses around the room. Never a drop was spilled. One sixpenny tip meant that he looked after you all night. A customer only had to nod and the repeat order was delivered in a flash. We even drank out of glasses. Only those who had been badly brought up would think of drinking from a bottle.

The no entry sign into Newland is now redundant. The whole area has been remodelled to make way for the Grosvenor Centre. Welsh House, to the right, though renovated, has survived. It had been in use as The Imperial Autocar Company Limited, a less than gracious occupation for such a historic building. The other fine buildings on the north side of Market Square gained no such stay of execution. Known as The Parade, they included the newspaper offices that had to report their own demise. This press building was a more recent addition to The Parade, coming along in the 1930s. Even sadder was the passing of the Emporium Arcade. This grand edifice had first opened for business in 1908. The array of building styles and ages gave The Parade an interesting look. The razing of them to the ground for the uniformity of the shopping centre is not a piece of history that Northampton people recall with any affection. The days of buildings that had features of architectural interest and individuality have gone. Instead we are in danger of creating town centres that could be moved from one place to another and no one would notice the difference. Where today can you see the intricate stonework and features demonstrated on the Emporium Arcade?

Left: It was a cold day, late in the 1950s. Everyone wrapped up in warm clothing. The more well to do women put on their best fur coats. The coats acted as a sign of success and were very cosy to slip inside. Attitudes have changed a lot in recent times. The green lobby pillories anyone donning real animal pelts. Animal rights seemed to become more important than human issues as we moved into a new millennium. Laboratories conducting medical research that used animals in their experiments were attacked. Rural communities were invaded by the anti foxhunting brigade. Lady Docker, the 50s' socialite, would have been egged today if she appeared in public under one of her array of mink coats. The centrepiece of the photograph was one of the glorious buildings that are no longer with us. It is a shame that there was no group called Friends of Architecture or Green Building in 1961 when the Queen's Head was knocked down. New office and shop buildings took its place on the corner of Gold Street and College Street. The Queen's sold Phipps' beers. The company offices were just further along the road. The family firm began brewing in Towcester in 1801. The operation moved to Northampton in 1817. Pickering Phipps was to serve as the town mayor in his later years, in 1860 and 1866. The company merged with the Northampton Brewery Company in 1957 and in 1960 with Watney Mann.

Above: The woman passing Central Hall was wearing the headscarf that became accepted as a covering in the 1950s. Ladies seldom went out with their heads uncovered. It was not the done thing. However, when no less a person than the Queen was photographed wearing a headscarf there was no need to search in the wardrobe for a hat. If it was good enough for Her Majesty then it was proper for we commoners to dress in similar fashion. The Central Hall, Abington Square, was once the Evangelistic Mission Hall. Its signboards were advertising men only meetings each Sunday at 2.50 pm. Perhaps the Mission believed that women were already guaranteed salvation. It had been founded in August 1875. The building's foundation stone was laid by Rev ET Prust on 15 July 1878. In later years Central Hall became the Irish Club. In more recent times it changed its name again, becoming The Centre nightclub. The sounds of DJs rapping the night away will probably make the Victorian evangelists turn in their graves. Raymond P Poole's shop next door sold baby carriages, toys and picture frames. The window display has attracted a little knot of shoppers. Notice that looking for baby things or kiddies' toys was a job for women. It was not considered manly for hubby to come along on such an expedition. It was just as well. He would only have got in the way. Poole's forebears once ran what was grandly called an optical show.

Both pictures: This was the day in the early 1960s that the statue of Charles Bradlaugh came to life. Fairies had sprinkled magic dust over his pedestal and the great man stepped down from the position he had held in Abington Square since 1894. Apparently the fairy dust was mixed with paint and he left his footmarks all the way from his base, across the road and back again. After 70 years in place it came as no surprise to find that he needed to use the toilet. Just to prove that he was as nonconformist as ever, he used the ladies'. That is the impression that the local art students wanted to give. It was their idea of a whiz of a rag week prank. Now sober citizens, some of whom are quite influential in the art profession, they might now look back on that time with a mixture of amusement and embarrassment. However, it was a hoot that caused no one any harm. It brought a smile to the faces of most of the population, even if there were some who muttered that they did not pay their taxes for youngsters to fool about. What they forgot was that rag week did a lot of good. Maybe there were some silly stunts and risqué jokes in the rag mag, but a lot of money was raised for charitable causes. Who were we to tut tut when a break from hard study brought such worthwhile results? All work and no play made Jack and Jill very dull boys and girls.

The Ovaltine poster, to the right of the statue, advertised the popular nightcap. 'We are the Ovaltinies' was the advertising song regularly played on Radio Luxembourg. The scooter turning behind the statue was a symbol of one group of modern youth in the 1960s. The other was the motor bike. Scooter riders, on brands such as Lambretta and Vespa, were known as Mods. Their bitter enemies, the Rockers, rode high powered BSAs and Nortons. The Mods favoured the new music of groups like the Small Faces, whereas the Rockers were firmly behind earlier stuff by Eddie Cochran and Jerry Lee Lewis. Their animosity spilled over into violence, especially on Bank Holidays at the seaside. Margate, Brighton and Clacton witnessed distressing clashes that ruined the day for families having a peaceful day out.

Bradlaugh was a free thinking radical, but he would not have approved of that sort of behaviour. His life was devoted to freedom, liberty and justice. He was a 'sincere friend of the people'. Bradlaugh would have approved of art students, but have drawn the line at Mods and Rockers.

Above: The photographer stood close to the Old Black Lion when he pointed his lens along Marefair. The pub gave its name to the hill on which he was standing. The former Gordon Hotel was on the corner of Chalk Lane. The buildings on the left hand side of Marefair have disappeared. Castle House has replaced those closest to the camera and, in 2001, the remaining section was still being developed. The railings on the right belong to St Peter's Church. It dates from 1160, but has even older connections with Saxon times. It is a fine example of Norman architecture that attracted the Greek Orthodox Church, to which it was loaned out for a while. Some of the intricate carving within the church is reminiscent of the decoration once found in the castle. Hazelrigg House stands beyond the church. Built in Elizabethan times, it was one of the few buildings to escape the ravages of the great fire of 1675 that destroyed much of Northampton. Oliver Cromwell is supposed to have spent the night there before the decisive Battle of Naseby when the New Model Army routed the Royalist forces. Marefair leads towards the junction with Horsemarket, part of the inner ring road system. This street now seems marooned from the rest of the town and its appearance has suffered as a result.

Below: Northampton probably has more green areas and pretty countryside nearby than most towns. Then there is the other side of the coin. During the reign of Queen Victoria the town prospered. Its population increased from 15,000 to 87,000. It grew at a gentler pace in the first half of the 20th century to achieve six figures. An injection of new industry helped Northampton's population to spurt on again until it stood in excess of 180,000 at the turn into the 21st century. Not everybody benefited from the 19th century growth. Housing conditions in parts of the Borough were pitiful. Families lived in cramped and unsanitary conditions. The tin bath on the back yard wall, next to the corrugated iron roof of the little poultry shed, is an indicator of what life was like for those without proper bathrooms. Hot water was heated in kettles and the bath taken down from its peg and placed in the front room. Washing day was a grind. The same bath was used to clean the family clothing. Women's hands were red raw by the end of the day. There was hardly enough room to peg out a fraction of the laundry. Indoors was just as cramped. Children shared bedrooms. Often they slept top to tail in the same bed. There was little privacy for their parents. The stress levels were high. The sound of raised voices frequently came through the walls. In the 1950s and 1960s high rise flats replaced the slum housing. They created their own problems. In many cases social deprivation merely moved skyward.

At Leisure

Wicksteed Foundry was one of the largest in the country. It specialised in the design and manufacture of equipment for children's playgrounds. The company built Wicksteed Park at Kettering partly as a benevolent gesture and partly to trial its equipment. It became a popular place for families to spend the day. There was plenty to keep them occupied. The park had boating lakes, a cycle racing track and miniature railway. In summer the extensive lawns were full of picnickers. Hampers of food were opened and tablecloths unfurled. The grub was washed down with homemade lemonade. Children squealed with delight as they played hide and seek or were gathered together for 20 a side cricket matches. The roundabouts, swingboats and seesaws attracted throngs of kiddies. The Wicksteed boffins carefully measured the popularity of use and the reliability of the equipment, particularly when viewing a prototype. The bandstand regularly echoed to the sound of Sousa marches and tunes from the musicals of the day. The best loved melodies of Gilbert and Sullivan were given regular airings. People came from many miles away, so well known did the park become. It was not somewhere to call in for a flying visit. Wicksteed Park became the Alton Towers of its day. The ornamental garden and bandstand are no more. Modern society wants big dippers and piped music. Just look at what it has lost. This park was a place for courting couples, families and senior citizens alike.

Far left: There are some adults who have a natural way with children. Kids can spot a phoney a mile away. That same intuition tells them who is the genuine article. Father T Aspell was such a person. This popular priest was not one who preached fire and brimstone from the pulpit. Although deeply religious, he recognised that there was fun to be had from life as well. Jesus had never said that the only path to heaven was via a glum route. He had scolded his disciples for trying to keep a group of youngsters from him. 'Suffer the little children' was his message. Father Aspell followed the same adage. He had come to share in the excitement of sports' day at St Mary's RC School. There were children clutching eggs and spoons and others with their legs tied to a partner. Obstacles were laid out for racers to clamber over. Parents lined the running track to watch the potato race. Instead of spuds the competitors collected little bean bags. They rushed backwards and forwards, put them in a bucket and then raced to the finish line. Then it was time for the fathers' race. The children told Father Aspell that, as he was 'a father', he qualified. He did not protest too much as he was hauled off to the start line. He won the race comfortably. The dads competing against him said they did not want to get too heavy a penance in confession, so they diplomatically let him win. Father Aspell told them they were guilty of the sin of pride and would be punished for that. They all laughed and made their way to the ice cream van.

Left: Where were you on 2 June 1953? Unless you were still a twinkle in the eye the odds are that you shared the day doing the same as these children. Linking Derngate and St Giles Street, Hazelwood Road is now home to solicitors, accountants and insurance offices. But, half a century ago, it was residential housing where this jolly group got ready to enjoy the day. As the Queen made her way to Westminster Abbey for the Coronation ceremony her subjects came onto the streets to join in the celebrations. There were processions and street parties, the like of which had not been seen since the end of the war. The day dawned damp and unseasonably cold. But the weather could not depress the nation's spirits. Wrapped up in warm coats, the children paraded in their fancy hats and wished Her Majesty well. Red, white and blue were everywhere and lads were happy to exchange their school caps for homemade patriotic ones. Perhaps these were the forerunners of the dreaded baseball caps. Despite the chilly conditions little boys and girls generally bared their knees to the elements in those days. Little white ankle socks were the common uniforms for the girls. Lads usually had longer grey socks, one of which was usually wrinkled and falling down.

England was on top of the world in 1966. The national soccer team, led by Bobby Moore, had won the World Cup, defeating West Germany 4-2 in a thrilling final, largely thanks to a Geoff Hurst hat trick. That summer was a scorcher. Children stripped off and plunged into the water to cool off. This was in the days before skin cancer scares fuelled the sun block industry. There was little protection for these bathers at Midsummer Meadow baths. Hardly anyone bothered with head covering. The sun was shining and it was great to turn pink and tender. On this day some 3,000 had come through the turnstiles by teatime. They frolicked in the warm water of the open air pool. The heating

came from the nearby generating station. The water the power station used was not discharged directly into the river. It was found that this damaged plants and wild life. Midsummer Meadow baths benefited as a result. They were popular with Canadian troops during the war. These servicemen were the subject of complaints that they were dominating the baths. As a

result the Canadians were restricted to Mondays for their recreation. The baths were also particularly popular with the locals: one enjoyed a daily dip, even in the coldest of weathers, until he was in his 80s. Midsummer Meadows went the way of so much of our entertainment of days gone by. The baths were filled in and the area turned into a car park

Above: In 2000 Frank Dobson was a Labour politician who threw his cap into the ring as a candidate for Mayor of London. He was well beaten to the nomination by Ken Livingstone, who went on to be successful in the election. That Frank Dobson gradually faded from memory. His namesake was a more influential man in the world of modern art. Sir Frank Dobson (1888-1963) unveiled his famous 'Woman and fish' sculpture in St Katherine's Gardens in May 1952. He spoke to the assembled crowd about his studies at the City and Guilds of London Art School. He reminisced about the times he had spent working with Cornish granite cutters. The French sculptor, Malliol, inspired much of his work. This Dobson example was heavily influenced by Malliol's 1936 bronze, 'Young woman Seated'. Local wags did not share the art world's appreciation of nude sculpture. They took every opportunity they could to decorate the woman with chamber pots on her head, a variety of bras on her chest and various unmentionables on her lions. The fish she held had a host of different matter issuing from its

mouth instead of the water that was supposed to gush forth. Tired of returning the sculpture to its original form on a frequent basis, the council had it moved to Delapre Park, away from the town centre vandals.

Top right: This happy family scene was caught in Wootton outside the 17th century cottage that Mr and Mrs Bernard Burgess and daughter Julie had bought. Bernard was a singer, but it was his wife who was the real focus of the photographer's interest. Officially Mrs Ruby Burgess she was

better known as Ruby Murray, the Irish songstress who had been the sensation of 1955. The Wootton cottage had been bought with the royalties from her record sales. Before the world had heard of Ireland's Sinead O'Connor or the Eurovision winner Dana, Northern Ireland produced an assault on the pop charts the like of which has hardly ever repeated. Just before Christmas 1954 she had her first hit record with 'Heartbeat'. The follow up single, 'Softly softly', went to number one and still gets airplay nearly half a century later. But Ruby was not finished with chart success. By the end of March 1955 she had released three more hits, 'Happy days and lonely nights', 'Let me go lover' and 'If anyone finds this I love you'. All five songs were in the top 20 at the same time, establishing her as an answer to trivia quizzes even today. Although Ruby's girl next door charm brought her further recording success and a series of sell out concert and variety shows, her star soon waned. Her last hit was in 1959 with 'Goodbye Jimmy goodbye'. Ruby's marriage did not last and she became something of a recluse, dying a forlorn figure on 17 December 1996: she was 61. Yet her name lives on in the most unusual of circumstances. These days youngsters go out to eat 'a Ruby'. Do they realise they are using the rhyming slang for curry that owes its origins to a frail singer popular with their grandparents?

Left: In the 21st century it is shaven heads that dominate the football field. Fashionable soccer stars of the 1970s sported flowing locks, kipper ties and lurched around on platform soles. Oh how the likes of Stanley Matthews and Tom Finney, victims of football's maximum wage, must have cringed. Soccer stars of the 1990s had money to burn, pop star status and the publicity that went with it. But, not everyone could handle the distractions of the bright lights. George Best was a prime example of how to waste a God-given talent. Easily the greatest British player of his time, he was on an international par with the Brazilian Pele and the German Beckenbauer. He burst on to the scene as a 17 year old with Manchester United in 1963. Part of the first English team to win the European Cup in 1968, the wheels began to come off. His drinking binges and man about town style brought him into conflict with his managers. Best reacted by going missing on several occasions. After playing on New Year's Day 1974, the 27 year old turned his back on top class football forever. What a waste. Later he reappeared playing for lesser clubs. The sharpness had gone, but his popularity remained. Here he is pictured at

Craven Cottage, where he was playing for Fulham in Division Two. On the left is Pat Crerand, a former United player who became Northampton's manager. Dave Bowen, the Cobblers' secretary is to the right. George had agreed to play for a Liverpool FC side in a testimonial match for Dave at the County ground. Best's reputation on and off the field could still pull the crowds in.

Below left: No one likes to be beaten. Even worse than that is a hammering. But for fans of the Cobblers a thrashing at the hands, or rather feet, of the mighty Manchester United became part of the history of both the club and all of English soccer. Northampton Town tasted glory in the 1960s. Promoted from Division Four in 1961, in 1963 the Cobblers were crowned champions of the Third Division, scoring 109 goals. Five players reached double figures, the top scorer being Alec Ashworth with 25 league goals in just 30 matches. Two seasons later Town finished runners up by just one point from champions, Newcastle United. The goalkeeper, Bryan Harvey, saved seven penalties during the season, including two in one match against Southampton taken by Terry Paine, England's penalty taker at the time.

Promoted to the top flight, the club spent 1965-66 rubbing shoulders with players who went on to lift the World Cup for England at the end of the season. By then the Cobblers' heady days were over. A County Ground record of 24,523 supporters

witnessed the penultimate home fixture with Fulham a 4-2 defeat. It relegated the club to Division Two. At least Barry Lines could boast that he was the first man to score in each of the four divisions. But, fate was not done with the club. By 1969 it had tumbled all the way back to the basement division. Then came 7 February 1970 and the fifth round of the FA Cup. Manchester United were the visitors. Coming off the back of a suspension, George Best ripped the defence to pieces. Here he is, collecting a pass from David Sadler, on the way to scoring one of the six goals he managed in an 8-2 victory for the Red Devils. The performance of 'El Beatle' was awesome. Goalie Kim Book had backache by the end, but a place in history was ensured.

Below: The van at the bottom of the picture belonged to A Watts & Son, the long established furnisher. It was photographed in front of the New Theatre in Abington Street. The theatre opened in 1912 when Rameses, an illusionist, was top of the bill. Although it had a brief flirtation with films after the second world war, it was basically a variety theatre. The first half of the 20th century was a great time for variety shows. They followed on the tradition of the old music halls, but were a more acceptable form of entertainment as they were less vulgar. Variety attracted audiences from across the board. There were all sorts of speciality acts. Dancers, animal trainers, unicyclists, jugglers and magicians all had their place. Top of the bill usually went to a singer or comedian. In the 1930s Gracie Fields and George Formby played to packed houses. Young comics like Arthur Askey learned

their trade there. The advantage of variety for comedians was that a well crafted act could be repeated up and down the country. Television put a stop to that. It demanded a swift turnover of material. The 'box' also rang the death knell for variety theatres. The New Theatre turned to nude shows in the 1950s in an attempt to revive its flagging fortunes. It was a forlorn exercise. In 1958 it staged its last show, 'Strip, strip, hooray'. That was a sad epitaph to a once great centre of entertainment.

Events and Occasions

Below: The town has had an affinity with the Salvation Army for a long time. It was not easy for the founder, William Booth, in Victorian times. He and his supporters were given a rough ride when they first came here. Their message that non-believers were bound to end up in hell did not go down well. Northampton folk were free spirits. They were used to working in a shoe trade that was a cottage industry. Each person played a part without being dictated to. Booth's meetings were often broken up in violent fashion. On one visit to the town the band was attacked. The big bass drum was burst and rolled off down the road. Gradually, Booth's support for the poor, alcoholics and the homeless won acceptance. His standing was enhanced when Edward VII invited him to his coronation ceremony. He became regarded with

affection and attracted a large following here. In 1934 his daughter Evangeline was elected as General of the Salvation Army. She attracted a large crowd to the Market Square when visiting Northampton. The band played a selection of rousing hymns and she spoke of her beliefs in helping those less fortunate than herself. Some of her ire was directed at the drinkers in the Queen's Arms. Formerly the Windmill, an early landlord, Christopher Gibson, was variously described as a musician, professor of music, teacher and fiddler! Evangeline concentrated on modern problems. She blamed many of society's problems on the demon drink. Money meant for feeding and clothing the family was passed over the bar counter. Men came home drunk, hit their wives and left the children hungry. Many of those listening knew that what she said was too often true.

Above: Queen Mary, wife of George V, was a frequent visitor to our county of spires and squires. In September 1937 she visited Brington Féte. Born Victoria Mary Augusta Louise Olga Pauline Claudine Agnes of Teck, she had been engaged to George's elder brother, Albert. He died a few weeks before the wedding ceremony and she married the future king in 1893. When she came to Brington she had been through a traumatic 18 months. Her husband had died, her eldest son had abdicated and her second child accepted the crown he did not really want. She handled it all gracefully. Queen Mary was a popular figure, but she could be an expensive one. Whenever she visited a place she usually spotted an object that took her fancy. 'I like that' meant that she expected it to be sent to her at Buckingham Palace. She built up several fine collections in that way. The boy on the left of the photograph should stir a few memories. Look carefully at his face and ask yourself where you have seen those features before. He was Edward John Spencer, father of Diana who became the Princess of Wales. Millions around the world shared the family grief when she was killed in a car crash in Paris in 1997. The little village of Great Brington is closed off every summer as the crowds pour into Althorp making a pilgrimage to Diana's memorial.

Below: The dapper 34 year old with the brilliantined hair strode out purposefully, furled brolly in hand. The neat handkerchief in his breast pocket and the cut of his suit announced that here was someone of class. You could not get more upper class than this. He was Albert Frederick Arthur George, Duke of York, but Bertie to his friends. Alongside him, wearing the mayoral chain of office, was Councillor Ralph Smith. The royal visitor had come to town during festival week, May 1930. General Hospital nurses provided the guard of honour. Although nursing had been part and parcel of a woman's lot, it was not until Victorian times that it became a recognised profession. Florence Nightingale, the lady with the lamp, was instrumental in effecting this change. In 1860 she established the first scientifically based nurses' training school at St. Thomas's Hospital in London. As the Duke of York passed between the ranks he could be forgiven if his mind were elsewhere. His wife was pregnant with their second child. Margaret Rose was due to make her entrance into the world in August. She would be a sister for the four year old Elizabeth. As the duke carried out his minor royal duties that day, little did he realise that he would be thrust into the limelight as King George VI. Nor could he have imagined that his elder daughter was destined to reign for half a century.

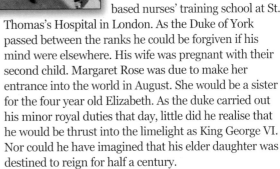

Above: Six battalions of the Northamptonshire Regiment gave noble service during the second world war. They were on coastal defence duties, fighting in Burma, engaged in Italy and to the forefront on the battlefields of North Africa and Europe. They fought bravely, but at a cost. Nearly 1,000 of their number died on active service. It is odd to see them listed as so many officers and men; as though it mattered to a grieving mother what rank her son held. 'In recognition of the glorious record of the Northamptonshire Regiment' it was awarded the freedom of the borough on 8 June 1946. The regulars and cadets marched proudly down George Row from the saluting base at the town hall. The crowds greeted them with heartfelt thanks as the parade passed

County Hall, the courts and sessions house on the right, built in 1682 to a design by Sir Roger Norwich. The building at the junction with Woodhill has changed little over the years. It is still serving coffee and tea as the Corner House. In earlier days the Clipper Café flourished in its oddly shaped basement. This was a spectacular establishment. Styled as the interior of an aircraft, it had aeroplane style seating and luggage lockers under its curved roof. The waitresses dressed as stewardesses and there were various round the world scenes to be glimpsed through the café windows. Had there been a fire the Clipper would have been a death trap. It was sad, but not surprising, that fire regulations forced it to close.

Carnival time was popular with everyone. In 1937 thousands lined the streets to watch the parade of floats making their way up Gold Street into George Row. It came as a welcome distraction from the worrying news from Europe. Fascist forces were on the march. Spain was gripped in the horror of civil war. Elsewhere Hitler and Mussolini were allying with each other. The storm clouds of war were gathering. At home we could escape by looking at the pretty girls in their costumes. They flanked the contraptions that had been gaily decked with garlands and bunting to set off the festive scene. Later there would be games and sports in the parks. The fairground would be alive with the noise of happy folk enjoying the dodgems, coconut shies and merry go rounds. In the meantime the crowd thrilled at the ingenuity of the float designers. The main one pictured was called 'Showboat'. It was an entry by the Rushden shoe company of John White Ltd. Not surprisingly, it won the championship cup. It was inspired by the 1927 Jerome Kern and Oscar Hammerstein musical. Paul Robeson's rendition of the show stopper 'Ol' man river' brought goose bumps up on the neck of anyone listening to it. Northampton's carnival had a long history. It began in 1890 as a cycle parade. At the time there were 12 cycling clubs in the town. The carnival raised funds for the General Hospital. After the war the birth of the NHS meant people were less inclined to give further financial support. It became more commercialised as firms used it to advertise their wares. As volunteer organisers became few and far between the carnival passed into history in the 1980s.

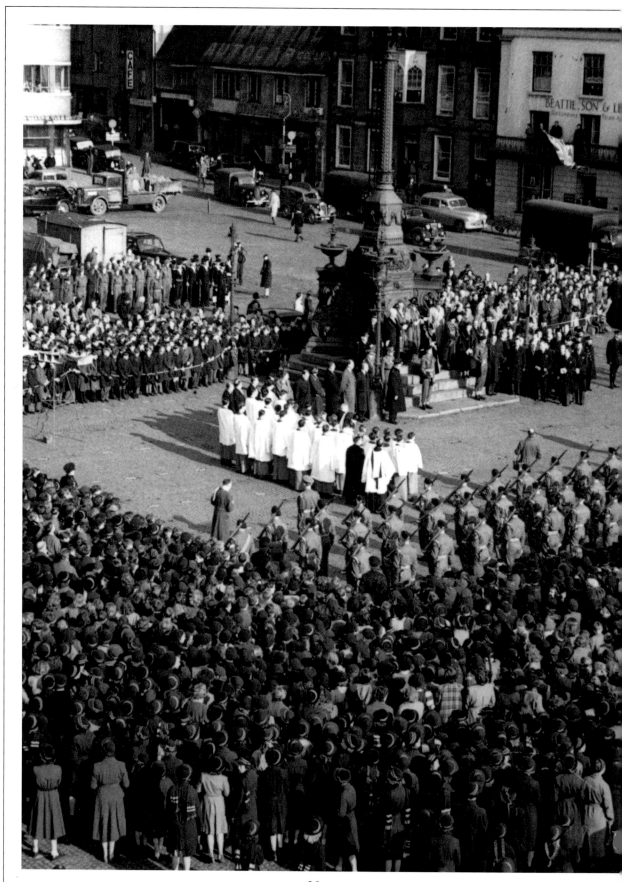

Left: The passing of a monarch is both sad and forward looking. It is the end of one era and the start of another. George VI began his reign in difficult circumstances. His brother, Edward VIII, abdicated at the end of 1936. That left an unprepared younger brother to take his place. The new king hated public speaking. His nervous stutter did not help. He was lucky to have the support of a strong wife, the former Elizabeth Bowes-Lyon. In later years she would become our beloved 'Queen Mum'. King George suffered from cancer. He died on 6 February 1952, aged just 56. The crowd in the Market Square paid homage to his passing as they listened to the proclamation of his successor, Elizabeth II. She was on a royal visit to Kenya when the news came through of her father's death. Mayor Frank Lee read the proclamation of her accession during a service held to mark the occasion. The country had taken the king into their hearts as he brought stability to a monarchy rocked by the antics of his brother with the twice divorced American, Wallis Simpson. They rallied again behind his young daughter who, at the age of 25, had to be the figurehead of a nation still recovering from the deprivations of the immediate postwar years. The proclamation was read in front of Beattie's auctioneers and the Peacock Hotel, a once famous coaching inn.

Below: Hands up if you want a coronation mug. The pupils at Stimpson Avenue School were about to give three cheers for Her Majesty as they gathered in the playground. They got their mugs in pretty little presentation boxes. Elsewhere Coronation crowns, worth a nominal five shillings (25p), were placed in plastic cases and pressed into outstretched palms. The coins were not for spending. They were wrapped in tissue paper and put away in the front room bureau. There they lay until the next time came for clearing out the drawers. Discovered again, they brought back memories of that happy Coronation day when we stood in neat, orderly lines and listened to the headmaster telling us about Queen and country. The mugs had a more central existence. They took pride of place on the mantelpiece, acting as a daily reminder that Britain is a monarchy. Some of the Stimpson Avenue children had come to school in their Brownie and Cub uniforms. The girls look very different from those of today, ever since Jeff Banks kitted them out in baseball caps. These days even children have to make a fashion statement. In the 1950s they put on short trousers or little dresses. School was a place to learn the basics and to enjoy being a child. They were disciplined enough to stand in rows and listen with respect. Even so, as can be seen from the cheerful faces, education was also fun.

Above: The young and not so young were having a whale of a time in Monks Park Hall. The tables creaked under the weight of the sandwiches, cakes and fancies that would soon be demolished by hungry gannets who needed no second invitation to enjoy themselves. The Union flags and gay bunting, flanked by colourful streamers, nicely set off the jolly scene. The notice board in the background has a Borough Honours List and next to it is a BOAC world map. The British Overseas Airways Corporation was founded on 24 November 1939. Imperial Airways and British Airways combined to create the new company that was to introduce regular transatlantic schedules in 1958, flying Boeing 707s. BOAC combined with British European Airways to form British Airways (BA) in 1974. By then the world had become a smaller place. Most of those enjoying the Coronation party in 1953 had no experience of air travel. By the time BA was formed Britons were looking towards airports as much as railway stations to take them off on holiday. Monks Park was part of an estate owned by a religious order in medieval times. Later, the house was taken over by Sir Henry Randall. It was replaced by a group of artisans' houses, surrounding this little community hall. In more recent times it became a chapel. It was popular with the Afro Caribbean community, but has since been knocked down.

Below: There is always someone around to go that bit further than anyone else. Every Christmas we put up our decorations. Somewhere nearby is a householder who takes that extra step. His house is festooned with fairy lights and giant Santas in the garden. George Rich was such a devotee of putting on a grand display. He designed the tableau that attracted the fancy of this group of children. The Coronation display was mounted in the front of one of the houses on Althorp Road. 'Long live the Queen' urged Mr Rich. She certainly did. Her reign extended into the 21st century. The children grew into middle age under her rule. Most of them were the product of the baby boom years. After the war there was a huge rise in the birth rate in the late 1940s. Servicemen returned from their time at the front. Unhappily, there was also an explosion in the divorce rate. Absence did not always make the heart grow fonder. However, for those families who were happily reunited nature took its course. The stork was overworked keeping pace with the number of deliveries he made. Althorp Road is in St James' End. The road name will always act as a reminder of the Spencer estate that is the resting place of the late Princess of Wales. St James' End was once a tiny village divided between the parishes of Dallington and Duston. Locals are known as 'Jimmies' Enders'.

Centre: Just off Towcester Road, the residents of Gloucester Crescent were making merry in support of the young Queen Elizabeth II. Already a two time mother, families could easily relate to her. Bunting that had been put away after VJ Day was unrolled and hung across the street. Large Union flags were draped across windowsills. Food for parties was prepared, but mums had to be careful with their rations. Some goods were still in short supply. Rationing was not to end completely until 1954. The folk of Gloucester Crescent did not let that stop them having fun. They gathered around the television owned by the posh family amongst them and listened to the melodious tones of Richard Dimbleby describing the Coronation scene. The flickering black and white images seemed quite magical, a technological wonder of the time. Back out on the street the music from the gramophones drifted out from open windows. Children joined in with Lita Roza's 'How much is that doggie in the window' and souls were stirred by the power of Frankie Laine's 'I believe'. They posed for this picture under one of the many celebratory arches that appeared in the town. This arch won a prize, seen here being proudly held. The castle holds centre stage on the shield. It acts as a reminder of the Norman construction destroyed in the 17th century on the King's orders. During the Civil War the town produced footwear for Cromwell's army. One order alone was for 2,000 pairs. Because of its support for the Roundheads, on the restoration of Charles II the town's castle was demolished. The motto on the coat of arms, 'Castello fortia concordia', keeps the memory alive.

Bottom: Thornton Park, Kingsthorpe, was just one of the many sites given over to the Coronation celebrations. It had once been projected as home for a new soccer stadium before being bought by the council in the 1930s. Note how patiently the children were waiting behind the line that they were not allowed to cross. There was no need to marshal them. They knew how to behave. The park was to be the scene of tea parties held in the Queen's honour. Little scones, potted meat butties, bread filled with the acquired taste of Heinz's Sandwich Spread and fairy cakes were scoffed at an alarming rate, all swilled down by glasses of fizzy cream soda or dandelion and burdock. Where do kids put it all? Before they were let loose on the food they prepared to wave their flags and streamers on sticks as processions and tableaux passed by. Then it was off to take part in the sports and games that had been arranged. Three-legged races, potato races and feet poking through the corners of various sacks were just as important here as the mile was to Roger Bannister or the marathon to Emil Zatopek. The little ones waiting patiently will be well into their 50s by now. Her Majesty has been with us so long that it will be these children's grandchildren who will be the little ones celebrating the next Coronation. God willing, it might even be their great grandchildren!

Below: Some addresses are better than others. Every town has an area that sounds more posh than most of the others. For Northampton, Delapre is one such place. Sometimes people who live just outside the district pretend that they live there. Image is all important. At least these folk living on Gloucester Crescent did not need to pretend. They lived within a stone's throw of Delapre Park, across the other side of London Road. The land for the municipal park came from 586 acres purchased from the Bouverie estate. From 1957 Delapre Abbey housed the Northamptonshire Records Office. But dry and dusty records were of no interest to these little cherubs. Squinting into the sun, they posed for the camera in a variety of fancy dress costumes. Mums had been busy, treadling away to stitch and sew some grand outfits.

Pirates crossed swords with guardsmen and majorettes vied with shepherdesses. After the photograph the children paraded before the street party judges. What a thankless task they had. They were the only ones who could not come out winners. Whoever they chose to receive the first prize was guaranteed to provide a family friend for life. On the other side of the coin they were about to make enemies of the other 25 in the competition. They learned their lesson. They never volunteered to be judges again.

Bottom: Off Wellingborough Road, not far from Abington Park, fancy dress was also the order of the day for children who lived on The Headlands. The Golden Coach was taking the newly crowned Queen to Buckingham Palace. London crowds were craning their heads to get a better look at the huge and beaming figure of Queen Salote of Tonga. But, back in Northampton, they had their own way of celebrating the glorious day. Mums had been busy stitching and sewing outfits for their children to wear. Dads had knocked together little carts to add to the fun. Then it was out onto the street to parade in toppers and national costume. Fancy waistcoats and brilliant bonnets were the order of the day. One little tot was so weighed down with all the flags sewn onto him that he was having trouble getting upright again after retrieving the stick he had just dropped. The girl sitting in the pram would later have it commandeered by her brother. He would turn into a racing machine. Soapbox derbies along the street and up and down the pavements saw youngsters pretending they were Juan Fangio or Stirling Moss. As they raced along the boys called out 'Brrm, brrm' in an attempt to sound like a Ferrari. Imagination played a great part in the way children entertained themselves. The Headlands pub nearby has a sign showing the cliffs and the sea. It was obviously painted to order by someone who had never set foot in the town.

Below: Just before the war some women wore their hair in styles that were fairly short, hugging the shape of the head. Others favoured a neat perm, with just a hint of wave and curl. The more flamboyant copied the flowing locks of such film stars as Rosalind Russell and Joan Crawford. In 1938, Picture Post and film magazines gave women plenty of scope to appreciate the variety of style available to them. Bebe Daniels, taking tea in the Derngate Café, seemed preoccupied with patting her own hair in place. She was with husband Ben Lyon. They were household names as stars of screen and radio. Theirs was one of the most successful of showbiz partnerships. Bebe was an experienced actress, appearing in over 300 movies. Ben took the starring role in the 1930

Howard Hughes film, 'Hell's Angels'. He was so big a name that Jean Harlow, the platinum blonde sex symbol, received second billing. The movie was nothing to do with motorbikes. It told the tale of two American pilots in the first world war. One of the first talkies, it was full of spectacular action and was reissued, partly for propaganda purposes, in 1940. Ben and Bebe made England their home during World War II. They had a hit radio show 'Hi Gang' with Vic Oliver, the first

guest on 'Desert Island Discs'. In the 1950s they included their children in an immensely popular family series, 'Life with the Lyons'. Bebe died in 1971 and Ben in 1979.

Below left: The children from Albert Street, along with parents and grandparents, got into the party mood. Even grandpa let down his hair and put on a silly hat. Well, why not? The last Queen to have been crowned reigned for over 63 years. It might be as long again before there was the chance of another similar do. This group had come to the nearest open space to its home. The yard of the fire station on The Mounts provided the chance to have a party and games in safety. The station was part of a complex erected by local builders in the mid 1930s. Designed by JC Prestwich and Sons, the fire station opened in 1935. Alongside it was a swimming baths and police station. The latter was built on the site of an old prison that closed in the early 1920s. The fire brigade moved to The Mounts from Dychurch Lane. It had bought its first motor fire engine in 1910, replacing the old horse drawn steam appliance. Three shiny new motors were housed behind the doors when the move here was made. It was to be hoped that there would be no emergency while this party was in full swing or there might be some squashed buns on the forecourt. The Albert Street residents would see their street flattened in later times. They were not run over by a fire engine but demolished as part of the Grosvenor Centre development.

Bottom: Local actress Freda Jackson was a member of Northampton Repertory Company. She went on to achieve fame, and some notoriety, in the 1948 movie, 'No Room at the Inn'. She played the cruel and monstrous character Mrs Voray. The storyline was quite adventurous for the era. It told of a woman who half starves evacuees and turns her house into a brothel. Such a hard hitting social theme was ahead of its time. Immediately after the war it was more acceptable to have films that told of thrilling deeds against all odds, delivered by our armed forces. They usually starred John Mills. 'No Room at the Inn' was based on a play by Joan Temple. It was in danger of being dismissed as a ridiculous melodrama. However, a full blooded performance from Freda ensured its popularity. She received top billing above such talented actors as Hermione Baddeley and Sydney Tafler. Freda Jackson was the wife of a famous local artist, Henry Bird. Here she was attending the opening of a display of royal photographs, 'Royal Occasion', in the company of Reginald Brown, the curator of the art gallery and museum. An old volume of the Chronicle & Echo had grabbed her attention. Freda attracted the interest of Hollywood. She received a number of offers to cross the Atlantic and try her luck in tinseltown. She turned them down as she was more interested in stage work. Freda returned to continued success in the theatre, even though a film career could have been hers for the taking.

On the Move

The wharf at Cotton End, just off Towcester Road, was used to unload barges coming down from Gayton Arm. They would have been filled with timber, grain and coal. The five mile length of canal was constructed to link the Grand Junction at Gayton with the River Nene. It opened up the town to canal traffic to and from the Midlands. The first loads were carried in 1815. The true canal era in England dates from the 18th century. James Brindley designed the Bridgewater Canal to carry the Duke of Bridgewater's coal from Worsley to Manchester. It opened in 1761, being extended to the Mersey in 1776. There then followed an intensive period of canal building, much of it interlinked across the country. Before the coming of the railways, barges were a cheap and effective method of transporting large quantities of goods and fuel. After rail and road replaced their usefulness many canals fell into disrepair. Greater leisure time saw conservation groups open up many old stretches in the late 20th century. Families took to the water for holidays, though they relied on diesel rather than horses to provide power. These barges tied up at Cotton End remind us of an age when movement around the country was conducted at a more peaceful pace. Bargees lay on their backs and used their feet on the tunnel roofs to help their vessels get through. Lads led the horses along pathways until the barges reappeared from the gloom. Driving 32 tonners bumper to bumper at 70 mph on the M1 is a different world

Above: Franklin's Gardens Hotel overlooks the land that had been requisitioned for war work. During World War II many open spaces and buildings were commandeered by the armed forces to provide bases for essential purposes. Northampton's famous rugby club first played as Northampton St James's Improvement Class Rugby Team, hence the nickname 'the Saints'. Franklin's Gardens, the home ground, was once gardens which included a bear pit. It has seen many games before and since those wartime years when the odd grizzly would not have seen out of place in the front row. When hostilities broke out on the battlefield the National Fire Service built on the flower gardens and old menagerie. Fire appliances and vehicles belonging to the Air Raid Precautions Service were housed there. Happily, they would not see the same level of use needed in the nation's major cities. But, just in case, Northampton had to be ready. Civil defence groups trained hard. They were ready to meet the challenge. Anti-tank barriers were erected. Bank managers and clerical workers swapped their suits for uniforms and took classes in assembling Sten guns and establishing emergency kitchens. When the bombs dropped the fire crews were well prepared to leap into action. They were anxious times, but the British were determined that the forces of evil would not prevail. If the call into action on the home front ever came, they were waiting. Today, the Saints can play in front of cheering crowds who owe their freedom to the sacrifices and preparations made during the war years.

Below: Not everything from Italy can be described as chic. This van did not have to whisper its presence or quietly suggest 'Stop me and buy one'. It positively screamed at you. The men examining its coachwork look as bemused as they ought to be. The vehicle, with its Borsani body, was built by the Italian OM company. The marketing department described it as being super streamlined. Others called it vulgar. Whatever your opinion it caught the eye when it arrived in Market Square and pulled up outside Church's China on the front of the Emporium Arcade. The chromework and the exaggerated fins were popular in the early 1960s. They aped some of the American styling on their large cars. A few of our own models, for example the Vauxhall Victor, were built along such lines. We may have thought they looked modern, but reliability let them down. The fins were water traps and some of the cars little more than rust buckets. The half wheel style of the rear wing was also used on the Citroen DS19. It looked smart but was a fiddly nuisance when trying to change a wheel. Quite what Thomas Church would have thought of the contraption in front of his shop window is anyone's guess. He, in company with son Wesley, opened his business in Northampton in the 1870s. The family firm, specialising in fine gifts, china and tableware, is unlikely to have approved of this sight glimpsed through its shop window.

Bottom: There was a time when we had to take it easy. Rush hour was a thing of the future. Britain was a land of leafy lanes and picturesque, idyllic scenes. Birds twittered on the branches. Now they cough in the morning as the exhaust fumes from internal combustion engines pollute the atmosphere. What was it like to travel at four miles an hour instead without another soul in sight? With progress comes loss. The gentleness of the countryside has disappeared under tons of concrete and tarmac. Even local residents will be shocked to realise that this is a spot over which many of them now race on a daily basis. It is Billing Mill Bridge. The bridge carries a large amount of traffic cutting through from the A45 to Brafield and the A428 Bedford Road. Visitors to the Billing Aquadrome use it all the time. The skew bridge takes its name from the old mill that stood close by. The millhouse has been converted into a pub, not surprisingly called Billing Mill. The wooden railings on the bridge have given way to a stone parapet. Apart from that change, it is as it was when this caravan eased its way across. If the modern driver could spare a few moments from his busy schedule, he would gain a lot from leaving his car behind and gazing at this spot for a short while. As the traffic thunders by, try to imagine how it would have felt to be clip-clopping gently over the water. Is life that much better for speed?

Birds Eye View

The aerial shot of the district around Foot Meadow, with St James' End to the left, was taken in the 1960s. Most of the area is now taken up by the industrial estate that would dominate any similar photograph today. West Bridge and Castle Station are in the centre of the photograph. On the left the fuel pipeline has been constructed at St James' Mill Road. The railway lines at the foot of the photograph are part of the lines that loop their way towards London and Peterborough. Thanks to the nonconformist Victorian attitudes of the 19th century the main line never reached Northampton. The stubborn attitudes did not want the town to follow others like sheep. Northampton wanted to retain its reputation for being individual. Some would call it quirky. It was even more surprising as the town had long prided itself as being the crossroads of England. Coaching routes that criss-crossed the countryside passed through Northampton, making it a transport hub. The growth of the industrial estate, to the southwest of the town close to the River Nene, is just one of the changes to the economic makeup of the town that took place in the last third of the 20th century. The traditional shoe and boot industry declined. New major contributors, such as Carlsberg, Avon, Barclaycard and Tesco, breathed new life into the town.

This aerial view of the gas works, with its gasholders dotted round like giant snare drums, shows the distinctive shape of Foot Meadow. The area nearby was known as Cotton Mill. This was not linked to the district of Far Cotton, but owed its name to a spinning mill that once flourished here. St James' Retail Park is now the main focus of this area. In the 1960s the first of the high rise flats can be seen putting in an appearance on the left. They were seen as a solution to the need to conserve space. The rising costs of building land contrasted with the comparative freedom of the sky. Developers adopted the supermarket

principle. Build them high, sell them cheap was applied to housing as well as stacks of baked beans. The effect upon the social lives of the residents only became apparent in later years. Changes would come to the railways, as well. The 1960s was a period of rail freight and passenger decline. The motorways took much of the traffic that had once been the monopoly of the railway. That brought its own problems as the country entered the 21st century. Pollution and overcrowding caused by lorries and motor cars are making us rethink attitudes towards transport. Whilst there is plenty of discussion, a solution seems as far away as ever.

Looking north across the town centre, the white block of the Debenhams' extension stands out, left centre. Near it is the delightful facade of the College Street Baptist Church, opposite Swan Yard. William Hull built the Nonconformist chapel in 1863. Behind there is a peaceful oasis of green. St Katherine's Gardens are on the site of a former church of that name. The Moat House Hotel has not yet appeared on the scene, so the photograph probably dates from the late 1960s. The Fish Market was just above Debenhams. It is now the town's covered market, but many locals still refer to it by its old name. The stalls in Market Square can be clearly seen in the centre of the photograph. The Emporium Arcade stood proudly above the market on the Parade. Welsh House is to its right. The Grosvenor Centre was later to take over much of this part of Newland. All Saints Church, lower centre, is at the elbow of road coming up from Bridge Street. As the road reaches its joint, Gold Street comes in from the left and the road changes to become the Drapery. The church has Mercers' Row to the north and George Row to the south. Northampton's first infirmary opened at 8-9a George Row in 1744. The undercroft within this building has links to medieval times. The building on the corner of George Row and Guildhall Road was once home to the officers from the County Gaol. It now houses the Tourist Information Centre.

Seen in the early 1980s Northampton skyline has changed dramatically since the developers had their way in the 1970s. The massive central area redevelopment is most marked to the right. It was in 1968 that Northampton was designated as a New town. The Northampton Development Corporation was formed to put the expansion plans into practice. They included areas outside the old borough boundaries. Within the town centre Northampton County Borough Council carried out its own complementary programme. Local authority offices were established in Northampton House, though they have now been dispersed to a variety of satellite sites around town. Other office blocks and multi-storey car parks were erected. The central shopping area around Market

Square was revamped. That is a polite way of saying that many buildings of character were sacrificed on the altar of progress. The Grosvenor Centre shopping complex opened in 1975, being fully completed a few years later. The £10 million Derngate Centre, to the bottom left, is a multi-purpose entertainment centre. The council opened it in 1983 on the site of the old United Counties bus station. Thankfully, Derngate still has a number of interesting buildings. There are houses from the Regency period. Bedford Mansions is an example of Art Deco from between the wars. Art Nouveau devotee, Charles Rennie Mackintosh, remodelled a 19th century house at 78 Derngate in 1916. St Giles Street runs up from the right hand corner of the photograph to meet Derngate at the Guildhall.

Northampton may be a form of inland port, having its own Customs post, but does it really need a lighthouse? There cannot be too many ocean going vessels making their way through St James' End. Of course there is not really a flashing light on top of this structure. There is no local equivalent of Inner Farne's Grace Darling rowing her way across the North Sea. This is the famous Express Lifts tower. Smith, Major and Stevens, an engineering firm from Battersea, made lifts and rope stranding machinery. Having opened a factory in 1909 on Weedon Road, it merged with Express Lifts in 1930. The Queen opened the 400 foot concrete tower in 1982. It was used as a test tower until the works closed in 1999. The huge factory has now been demolished. The area has been redeveloped for good class residential housing. The friars of St James' Abbey once owned the land. An archaeological dig exposed the abbey's foundations. Some 200 burials were uncovered, including one of a nobleman or knight. The Northampton 'lighthouse' provided him with one of the world's tallest tombstones! Its fate has prompted much discussion. One idea has been for it to be turned into a restaurant along the lines of London's Post Office tower. It is fortunate that its future was discussed in the 21st century. Were this the 1960s or 1970s it would have been bulldozed without a second thought. It might not be pretty, but it is a period piece

On the home front

During both world wars there were constant fundraising drives as part of the war effort. There would be tank week, aircraft week and battleship week. This was a warship week in 1940. Crowds clustered on Market Square to show support for those risking their lives on the high seas in defence of the nation. Britain was not as well prepared for war as she might have been. Too many people accepted the prime minister's assurances that he had gained a promise of peace from Adolf Hitler in September 1938. Neville Chamberlain will forever be remembered as the gullible soul waving a slip of paper that pledged 'Peace for our time'. Less than 12 months later a Wehrmacht force of 1.25 million swept into Poland. In May 1940, during a Commons debate, the Tory MP Leo Amery told Chamberlain, 'In the name of God, go!' He did and in came Churchill. In the 1930s he had warned that Britain's defences were weak. The population listened to his rallying call and strove to make up for lost time. They opened their purses and poured their hearts and souls into the war effort. The mock-up on Market Square, presided over by the First Lord of the Admiralty, AV Alexander, quaintly dressed in the uniform of the Royal Yacht Squadron, yielded excellent results. The town adopted HMS Laforey. The connection is still remembered by the annual Laforey parade and a memorial in the town hall.

Above: These folk look like something out of a 'Dr Who' programme or from a 'Star Trek' film. The gas masks may look funny to us but they were donned very seriously during the war. Men and women working for the local authority and auxiliary personnel were issued with their personal defence equipment in case the enemy used gas or germ warfare as a weapon. A typical gas mask consisted of a tight-fitting facepiece containing filters, an exhalation valve and transparent eyepieces. Special ones were manufactured for toddlers. The fear of chemical warfare was very real. During the first world war the Germans infected Romanian cavalry horses, as well as livestock in the United States destined for shipment to the Allies, with glanders. This was a virulent bacterial disease, producing horrid lesions. Chlorine gas was used on Allied troops at Ypres in 1915. Later in the war both sides used phosgene and mustard gas. The government feared that gas or germ bombs could be dropped on the population. That they were never used was due to fear of similar reprisals. But, just in case, civil defence groups trained in simulation sheds such as this one specially put up on the fire station yard at The Mounts. The notice pinned on the door was an unhappy prediction of something the world would discover as the war came to an end. Six million Jews perished in the gas chambers of Nazi death camps.

Below: Even in 1944 normal life continued. Buses trundled up the street and women indulged in window shopping. Clothing was rationed. Material was needed for uniforms, army greatcoats and parachutes. Mums got out the sewing machine and turned curtains into frocks. Petrol was restricted to essential use and cars were put into mothballs until the end of the war. As best we could, we tried to carry on with our normal routines. However, the shelter on the Drapery reminded us that, however hard we tried to forget, there was still a war on. At first sight this one looks like a Tardis, that miraculous time travel contraption that was a hundred times larger inside than out. The shelter could take 70 people, according to the sign on top. Where would they all fit? Was there some magic shrinking powder inside that reduced the occupants to the size of ants? The answer is boringly simple. A labyrinth of old cellars and vaults ran under the town centre. This box covered just one of the entrances. Similar structures were dotted all around the centre, giving speedy access to underground safety in case of an emergency. The stories that people told after their time beneath the Drapery pavement gave rise to legends about secret tunnels. Fanciful storytellers conjured up images of hooded monks, secret lovers and smugglers making their way along the winding passages.

The Air Raid Precautions (ARP) rescue vehicle had been pressed into service collecting metal. The ARP was one arm of the civil defence staffed largely by those in exempted jobs and volunteers too old or too young to join up. The Women's Voluntary Service, Local Defence Volunteers, St John Ambulance and a host of other groups who rallied behind the flag, supported their work. As the war went on valuable resources were in danger of becoming exhausted. German U boats blockaded our island, attacking merchant shipping trying to bring the raw materials needed to replenish our stocks. As more ships, aeroplanes and tanks were needed to advance our progress in the war, so every piece of available metalwork was commandeered.

Park railings were ripped down. Wrought iron gates disappeared and even kitchenware was pressed into service. These ARP men were dismantling iron railings from the corner of Spencer Parade, near the statue of Edward VII and the hospital. The intricate work of the ironsmith had to be sacrificed in the interests of our freedom. The scrap would be melted down and recycled to manufacture another Spitfire, cruiser or Centurion. It was a cheap price to pay for our future security. The workmen knew that they were doing their bit for king and country. The sweat on their brows meant more firepower for those at the front. The efforts of the ARP helped bring the war to a successful conclusion. It was not all down to those in uniform.

Right: It was warm work under the summer sun. Unlike their modern counterparts these fellows kept their shirts and waistcoats firmly in place. Nor was there any sign of their trousers slipping below their waists to reveal an unsightly backside. Some of these men had seen trenches before. They had suffered on the Somme, at Mons and by the Marne. Veterans of the Great War they turned their hands to preparing for the next international conflict. In 1939 we had come to realise that Hitler only meant to conquer, not appease. Belatedly, Britain prepared for war. The trenches being dug on the racecourse were not meant to hold fighting men. They were part of the preparations for underground shelters. These ones were made by Bell's, a local fireplace firm. Constructed of prefabricated concrete, they had been commissioned as a response to the Spanish Civil War. Military experts had seen what had happened at Guernica in 1937. The Basque cultural and spiritual home was flattened by German Heinkels and Junkers sent to help General Franco. The aeroplane versus innocent citizens was no match. The War Ministry recognised that air power would be a major force in future conflicts. Shelters were hurriedly put in place to protect the public. Air raid practice sessions were held. Individuals built shelters in their own gardens, stocking them with tinned food and candles. Cellars were cleared and furnished. In the capital Londoners practised sheltering in the underground tube stations.

Bottom: Who would think that a highly tuned fighting machine might evolve from this pile of scrap? This was the result of just one of the many salvage weeks that punctuated the war. As raw materials became increasingly in short supply all hands went to the pumps to produce waste and unwanted goods that could be recycled. Competitions were held between towns to discover which one was the champion scavenger. That appealed to the townspeople's sense of civic pride. Churches and town halls sprouted thermometers that charted the progress of the salvage drive. Books were pulped. Bones were ground down. Rags were collected. Pots and pans were donated, old tyres removed from lorries and bikes. Bedsprings were tossed onto the collecting carts. Church railings were torn down. All this was to help the war effort. Volunteer groups set up collecting stations in church halls and schoolrooms. They sorted through what might have been classed as junk. It was hard to imagine that the Hurricane flying overhead owed its existence to iron, aluminium and rubber collected and stored at the West Bridge depot. The man in the centre of the scrap seems lost in reflection. Perhaps he was wondering just how to begin sorting this heap into some sort of order. Maybe he was giving thanks for the ingenuity that could transform a pile of rubbish into something that was going to see active service in the defence of the realm.

Below: The war brought many overseas divisions and foreign volunteers to our shores. Poles, Free French, Ukranians, Americans and Commonwealth personnel flooded here. A large contingent of Canadian troops was billeted in Northampton. When the balloon first went up in 1939 many families were panicked into sending their children away from the cities. They sought the safety of the countryside and smaller towns as evacuees during Operation Petticoat. Northampton took in over 15,000, including some Jewish refugees from Poland and Germany.

After war was declared a period of quiet, referred to as the phoney war, took over. By the spring of 1940 parents were missing their children and the youngsters were homesick. Most returned home. Before long the blitz on our cities was under way and some evacuees returned. The children in this picture might have included some of them amongst their number. They were pestering a Canadian soldier for a handout of chocolate or chewing gum. Northampton residents were puzzled that their allies from across the big pond seemed to have a never ending supply of

cigarettes and sweets. There was some animosity between Northampton youth and the soldiers. The overseas troops were better paid than the Tommies and could turn a girl's head with presents of nylons and perfume. They loved to spin exaggerated yarns. Each one claimed to be a champion at something, usually boxing. 'Overpaid, oversexed and over here' was a constant grumble about the Americans and Canadians. However, it is a fact that without their input our little island would have been crushed under the jackboot of Fascism.

Bottom: There were seven in the bed and the little one said, 'Roll over'. The little lad does not look too unhappy about being turfed out. Although not as snug as a bug in a rug at least he and his pals were safe and sound. They had sought protection in one of the many vaults under Market Square. If the aeroplanes dropped their high explosive from above then they should be all right deep in the bowels of the earth. The bunks were fairly spartan, but the children were not likely to spend much of their time asleep. For them, this was an adventure. They were too excited with the novelty of the experience to get any shuteye. As time went by they entertained each other with stories of ghouls and ghosts wandering unchecked in the underworld to which they now belonged. The girls squealed in mock horror as the mischievous lads embellished their tales with bloodthirsty details. When the all clear was given they left their temporary home with some regret. They had taken part in an adventure. Their parents were amused to learn that they really had seen a man walking the vault with his head tucked under his arm. In their dreams they had also discovered secret passages to Delapre Abbey and Northampton Castle. After the war the roads above collapsed from time to time. The weight of increased traffic was too much for them to bear. Some of the vaults into which they collapsed were three storeys deep.

Above: Northampton can count itself lucky. It suffered little from the bombing raids of the Luftwaffe during World War II. Try telling that to the owners of the bungalows near Bants Lane. Their homes disintegrated. The tin hat hanging from the bicycle was little protection against the stick of bombs that created such havoc. Northampton's first experience of the mayhem came in August 1940 across Duston and St James' End. Although only 38 bombs landed on the town, one was enough if you were underneath it. A fire warden was killed when he came across what he thought was a fizzing bomb. He did not realise that the noise was coming from a damaged power cable. When he squirted it with his stirrup pump the poor chap was electrocuted. Only those of us drawing a pension can remember those terrible wartime days. People speak cheerfully of the bulldog spirit of the British, whistling 'We'll meet again' through six years of hostilities. They forget the nights of fear when the planes droned overhead. The anxiety of waiting for them to pass over was an almost as bad as the shock of when the bombs fell. For those in the big cities it went on night after night. The nation displayed a steely determination, but nerves were stretched to breaking point. Those hit in the raids lost their homes and prized possessions. They had to start all over again.

Below: This young couple put a brave face on it. Mr and Mrs Faulkner lived on Duston Road. Theirs was one of the houses destroyed in the 1940 bombing raid. The power and heat of the blast turned the stained glass window from their front door into a twisted lump of metal. At least they escaped without injury. It was upsetting to lose their home, but they had each other from whom to draw strength. Bricks and mortar could be rebuilt, but lives could not be restored. They were two of the lucky ones. Students today will have read about or seen films and documentaries about the war. They will know of the sacrifices made by our brave aircrew. The land battles and losses at El Alamein and the killing fields of Europe are common knowledge. They will be well acquainted with the stories of those lost at sea. But does the country really appreciate what it was like to be part of the blitz on Britain's towns and cities? The Faulkners walked away, but 92,000 civilians perished from the hail of death that rained from the skies. Those at home were just as much at the front as those fighting overseas. On a lighter note, some of the bombs that missed Duston Road landed in the cemetery. One tombstone was blasted high into the sky. It fell through the roof of a house, coming to rest on a bed close to one very startled resident.

Shopping Spree

The view along Bridge Street was taken with the photographer's back to St John's RC Church, founded in 1138, close to the former infirmary. St John's Street is the cobbled thoroughfare leading away to the right. The line of cars parked along Bridge Street shows how dependent we had become on the petrol engine, even in the 1950s. Car ownership had once been the privilege of the middle class. After rationing came to an end and we passed through the 1956 Suez crisis, a new period of affluence dawned. There were plenty of jobs around. The order books of businesses were full. The feel-good factor, lost during postwar austerity, returned with a vengeance. The motor car became almost a family necessity. Electrical goods revolutionised the kitchen. Monday washday blues became a thing of the past as the laundry spun inside a machine. The mangle and dolly tub were consigned to the museum. Motor cycling became a popular pastime for that new consumer group, the teenager. Coldham's was a long established two wheeler dealer. Business boomed as young men tried to impress their girlfriends with riding skills copied from Geoff Duke. They dreamed of being the first to average a ton in the Isle of Man TT, a feat that would be achieved in 1960 by Derek Minter on his Norton. Coldham's came to a dramatic end. The shop collapsed whilst building work was taking place next door. Fortunately, the incident happened at night and no one was hurt.

Above: During the years around the war money was tight. Even so, men still wanted to dress as elegantly as they could afford. Henry Price, who only died in 2000, spotted a niche in the market. He established his Fifty Shilling Tailors, selling cheap, but acceptable, clothing. Soon he had a chain of stores across the country. His outlet in Northampton stood on the corner known to old Northamptonians as Doffman's Corner. It was named after the firm of tailors that had been on the site before Henry Price came to town. It is one of the town's oldest buildings. Subject these days to a protection order, it should have many years left in it. It is regrettable that some of the other fine buildings nearby were not given similar help before the demolition men moved in. Looking up Abington Street from Mercers Row, Wood Hill is to the right and Market Square away to the right. Burton's, on the opposite corner from the Fifty Shilling shop, was a more upmarket competitor. The Belisha beacons around Doffman's Corner were a necessary indication showing pedestrians where to cross the road in some safety. Traffic negotiating this crossroads had become more congested and hazardous. The first pedestrian crossings were introduced in Britain in the 1930s. Plans were made to copy a successful Parisian experiment. Leslie Hore-Belisha was the minister of transport given the job of overseeing the changes. He was the Secretary of State for War when hostilities broke out in 1939. However, his name has forever been linked with the flashing beacons he introduced.

Bottom right: The buses passing the County Café in the Alexandre building approached Doffman's corner from Mercers Row. The passengers smoking on the top deck of the leading bus would have been keen to sniff the air outside S & G tobaccos. The smell of sweetly aromatic Turkish and Virginian mixture wafted up from the trays and display cases inside. If ever there was an excuse for having a drag on that foul weed, this was it. The devil does not only have the best tunes, he has some pretty good aromas as well. The bobby on point duty had his hands full at this busy intersection. Even in the 1950s it was something of a bottleneck as the rise in car ownership rocketed. The bus coming from Abington Street had already negotiated one difficult trouble spot at Abington Square. This junction was also dangerous to cross, being offset into Wood Hill. The photograph was taken from All Saints' church and the opening into Conduit Lane can be made out alongside the café. As might be guessed from the name, this was where the town's first water supply arrived, having been brought from springs on the outskirts. Doffman's tailoring store was so well known that the corner was named after it. Even when the firm no longer traded people still called it

Burton's tailors held pride of place on the corner where Woodhill meets Mercers Row and the bottom end of Abington Street. The well known store, founded by Montague Burton, gave rise to a number of expressions in common use in the 1950s. 'You are so lucky that if you fell off Burton's roof you would land in a new suit' was one of them. 'Don't stand there like some dummy in a Burton's window' was another. The most memorable related to men getting their demob clothing after the war. Going for 'the full Monty' referred to a whole new outfit. The expression was used for the title of a popular film of the 1990s, though the script dealt with disrobing rather than the opposite. The HSBC bank and Skipton Building Society now use the premises. Drum Lane, the little opening to the left, was once known as Drury Lane. It leads through to Market Square. George's Parlour, a pleasant place to stop off for morning coffee, stood on the corner. If the tables were taken then there was the Geisha just a little further along. Anyone wanting to buy something stronger could pop into Lankester and Wells, the wine merchant in the Royal Exchange Assurance building. Just in case of over indulgence a visit to Timothy White and Taylor to top up the Alka Seltzer was recommended.

Doffman's Corner. Saul Doffman, a man who gave some time in public service as a councillor, was the founder of this Jewish family business. Spoor and Son, a rival tailor and gent's outfitter, stood on the opposite corner. Mrs Spoor used to be a regular sight in the upstairs window. She seemed to spend much of the day there, gazing regally down on all that happened beneath her. A grand lady, she became something of a tourist attraction. Ironically, the two rival businesses gave way to the Fifty Shilling Tailor and Burton's. The owners changed, but the trade and competition continued as before.

Below: In the 1960s the shoppers were out in force on Abington Street. It was a time of pacamacs and rain hoods. Kiddies wore bobble hats and wrapped up in duffel coats. They never could manage those difficult to fasten toggles. The frontage of the shops showed a variety of styles, linking the old and the new. The attractive rounded cupola belonged to Phillips' drapery store. It is now an even busier spot. Although people still use it as an important retail area the look has changed dramatically. It is now pedestrianised and the new shopping centres have replaced the outlets seen here. It used to be a busy and congested thoroughfare. Shoppers had to be wary of the traffic and there were a number of accidents on the occasions that the traffic actually moved. The Peacock Centre is now on this north side of Abington Street. Peacock Place provides a connection through to Market Square. In 1986 a belated attempt was made near here to acknowledge Northampton's traditions in the footwear industry. A modern sculpture was placed by the entrance to the Grosvenor Centre, close to Fish Street. The Northampton Statue shows two children playing on top of a large last. It is the work of Graham Ibbeson and is, at least, a reminder that children once wore something else other than training shoes.

Right: This section of the south side of Abington Street has changed little in over 40 years. Traffic is now banned, but the buildings still stand proudly overlooking the townspeople busying along the pedestrianised way. The number of cyclists in the photograph show how popular that form of travel used to be. In recent years the humble bike has made something of a comeback as workers try to find an easier and more healthy way of beating the traffic jams that surround the town in the rush hour. The congestion has been removed from the town centre. Unfortunately, it has just shifted to the arterial routes. The building to the right is home to the Co-op. A Watts & Sons, established in 1896, is still there, just beyond the zebra crossing. The darker building in the centre is home to Northampton Central Library. It is only just part of Edwardian architecture as it dates from 1910. It was largely built with contributions from the American steel magnate Andrew Carnegie. The town councillors initially refused his money. They objected to his refusal to accept the rights of trade unions. Carnegie was born in Scotland. He helped found many educational trusts in his homeland. He believed that those with wealth had a duty to help others. He is thought to have donated £350 million to good causes during his lifetime. In Northampton common sense eventually outweighed principles and the donations were accepted. The library's local studies area is called Carnegie Hall in his honour.

This clever elevated view of Market Square was taken in the late 1960s from inside the clock that stood above the old Emporium Arcade. When the arcade was demolished the clock was preserved. It is about all that remains of the buildings that made way for the Grosvenor Centre. When this photograph was first printed the clock numbers appeared the right way round. The sub-editor thought he was doing the right thing. Fortunately the mistake was spotted before publication. Looking from the back of the clock, of course, the numerals should be back to front. The market stalls below are still flourishing. There are now even more stalls instead of the cars that were parked there over 30 years ago. Life on market days is all hustle and bustle. But it is friendly and enjoyable activity. Banter from the stallholders continues to amuse and entertain shoppers. The cheeky chappies have time to chat with their customers whilst conducting a brisk trade. It is an art form and part of the rich pattern of Northampton life as it used to be. Try holding a conversation with the check out girl in the supermarket and she will have you arrested for harassment. Looking south across the square, the attractive tower of All Saints rises above the town. The church was built in 1680, replacing the 11th century building destroyed in the fire of 1675.

Making a living

Below: Where have all the characters gone? At one time every town and village boasted people who were well known and loved for the individual stamp they placed on life. Perhaps we have become too easily cloned as neat round pegs in circular holes. Here is a couple who stood out from the crowd. They broke the mould where the Paynes were concerned. The father and son team of chimney sweeps was a dearly loved pairing in the town. They lived at 55 The Green in a little terraced house. Covered with sea shells, it stood as an oasis in a desert of rubble for many years. The Paynes defied a compulsory purchase order on the house and continued to live there as their neighbours' homes fell under the swinging ball of the demolition men. Every summer the elder Mr Payne could be seen punting along the River Nene. His portable radio played softly as he enjoyed the lazy, hazy, crazy days of summer that Nat 'King' Cole sang about. It was only after his death on 2 July 1963, at the age of 80, that the developers had their way and pulled down his house. Mr Payne had triumphed as one against the might of authority. Perhaps, in that great chimney in the sky, he is still using his brushes to clean up for St Peter. Alongside him might be the little boys who once went up the chimneys in Victorian times. Charles Kingsley's 'The Water Babies' highlighted their dangerous and difficult job. Published in 1863, it helped raise awareness of the terrible nature of child labour.

Above: These boots are made for walking. They were also made for dancing, fashion wear, working, running and everyday use. If not just boots, then shoes as well. This was the closing room at Barratt's. The boot and shoe industry has its own language, as do other industries. Pottery workers have their saggers, textile workers their teasels and miners eat their snap. Closing meant finishing off the shoe above the welt by stitching together the uppers. In 1931 Britain was suffering from a depression in employment. It hardly looks to have hit Barratt's. The company was one of the first to embrace the mail order business. A customer drew round his foot onto a piece of paper and sent the pattern to the appropriately named Footshape Works. The drawing was used to provide accurately fitting footwear. Nearly all of those in this room were women. In those days there was still a division between what was regarded as men's and women's work. There was a division in wages as well. If a woman abandoned the kitchen sink then it was only to come out to earn pin money. Society had forgotten how women had kept the country running in the 1914-18 war: they handled heavy machinery, drove tractors and did everything a man could. Yet, here they were, back doing 'women's work'. Although husbands were very happy to see extra cash coming in, they still wanted the house cleaning and tea on the table. A woman's work was never done. Barratt's recognised its responsibility to the community, donating money for the building of a maternity home. 'Walking the Barratt way' became slang for being pregnant. The company became part of the Leeds based Stylo group in 1964.

Below: For 60 years British Timken has been one of Northampton's major employers. The Birmingham based manufacturer of roller bearings opened a branch factory at Duston in March 1942. Britain's major cities were under attack from German bombing raids and it was wise to disperse some of the country's vital manufacture to quieter areas. This photograph, taken in January 1960, shows what appears to be a happy, cheerful workforce. Although they were putting on a smile for the camera, the workers were actually on strike. They had gathered to listen to shop stewards' recommendations for future action. This was in the time of high employment under the Macmillan government. It had won the general election three months previously with a thumping majority on the back of the slogan, 'You've never had it so good'. Two women, wearing the typical headscarf of the time, standing together near the cars in the centre, would take special interest in a Macmillan speech later in the year. He harangued the South African government for its apartheid policy in his 'Wind of change' address in Capetown. The women in the photograph were part of a small Afro Caribbean community living in Northampton. By the end of the century there would be a much larger representation of various ethnic minorities. In recent times these included refugees and immigrants from the Balkan conflicts. The cultures brought with them new ideas in fashion, cuisine and business as they helped mould the new Northampton.

Centre: Here is a source of annoyance to most of Northampton's 50 plus brigade. The demolition of the fountain on the Market Square on 15 April 1962 continues to make the hackles rise on those of a certain age. It should make younger ones equally irate. A part of the town tradition was lost forever on that fateful day. At least older residents have their memories of the structure. Anyone under 40 will never have had the opportunity to see it first hand. A local shoe manufacturer, Samuel Isaacs, erected the fountain in 1863. It stood as a tribute to the marriage of Albert, Prince of Wales, with Princess Alexandra of Denmark. Albert would eventually become Edward VII. The fountain often acted as a backdrop for speakers, protestors and politicians wishing to address the crowds. There was also plenty of heckling to accompany the speeches. In its wisdom the council decided that the structure was in a dangerous condition. Instead of repairing it, council workmen were instructed to remove it. If it was so rickety why did it take a team of men two days with cutting torches to bring it down? To compound the crime the fountain was lost forever. It was not even put into store, but disposed of as just so much scrap. In 1962 Leicester Permanent Building Society, Abel's Records (a music shop since 1790) and the Emporium Arcade occupied the buildings in the background. To the left, the Gaumont was showing a feature starring Joan Collins and Bob Hope.

Bottom: The New Theatre would not get any older. Its demise was ugly. The popular variety centre closed in 1958 and was demolished in 1960. The diggers and bulldozers from Northants Plant Hire swept away the boards trodden by household names of entertainment who had appeared here since December 1912. But, the memories and enjoyment we gained from our time in the stalls lived on. The music and fun of Sid Millward and his Nitwits, the flying feet of the Clark Brothers and the bunches of coconuts brought by the Billy Cotton Bandshow echoed around the grave of the New theatre. We shall draw a veil over the girlie shows that blighted its final years. The rafters had once rung to the sound of 2,000 pairs of hands applauding the stars of radio and variety. Next, these hands would be pushing supermarket trolleys around the site. Later still it became a clothing store. The frieze above the archway was part of the intricate decoration of mythological Muses and other figures. Dr Reynolds, a local historian, was able to salvage it. He used it as a mural in his terraced house. He displayed it on the wall that led from downstairs all the way up to his bedroom. Some time later, in a bizarre burglary, thieves stole the mural. The motive behind the theft still puzzles the police.

model T class, built by Henry Ford. The cars he built in 1908-27 were nicknamed 'Tin Lizzies'. They were cheap and affordable, though a somewhat bumpy, rattling ride. The truck version was built along the same lines. Ford opened an assembly plant in Manchester to widen his network. The scaffolding rising high above roadway was in place for the 1925 erection of the Westminster bank. The site had previously been used for a variety of purposes. The County Fire Office, a patent medicine shop and a seller of false teeth had been based there. The bank building was topped off with a copper dome, 45 feet in circumference. It once gleamed brightly across the town, but has become tarnished with time. Still dealing with money matters, it is now occupied by the Nationwide instead of the Westminster.

Top: The College of Technology on St George's Avenue underwent development in 1961. For many years the premises had a hollow U shape. The girders, scaffolding and cranes came together to enclose what had always seemed to be an incomplete structure. The 1960s was just one of the many decades that brought great changes in education. Snootier universities began to open their doors to working class students. Further education was actively encouraged so that youngsters looked to continue their education rather than rush off into a menial job. Future prime minister James Callaghan produced an impassioned report in favour of comprehensive schooling and an education broader than one offered by traditional academic subjects. The Labour government encouraged the dropping of the 11 plus exam. Children form different backgrounds and of varied abilities were schooled together. By the 1970s discovery methods of teaching had replaced rote learning. Education became a vote winner long before Tony Blair swept to power in 1997 with his slogan 'Education, education, education'. Margaret Thatcher had already used public interest in schools to help her gain high office. She was the first Secretary of State for Education ever to progress to the country's top political job. The changes continued in the 1980s and 1990s as attitudes hardened against laissez faire styles. Rigorous testing for youngsters came back into vogue. Now renamed Nene College St George's Campus, the college continues to evolve, hoping to achieve university status.

Above: The tramlines curving across the corner of the Drapery and Mercers Row only carried electric trams for 30 years in Northampton. By 1934 they had carried their last passengers as buses began to dominate public transport. Two examples of popular vehicles can be seen to the left. The motorbike and sidecar had a lengthy life. Although a dangerous contraption in an accident, particularly for the vulnerable passenger, it was a common sight on our roads for most of the 20th century. Even the motoring organisations took it on board. The AA and RAC patrolmen used to ride around on them, using the sidecar as storage space for emergency repair kits. Remember how the riders saluted a member as he drove past? The practice was banned for reasons of safety. It had been a nice touch of politeness. We could do with more of it. The truck belonged to the

The Esso sign means happy motoring. That was one of the slogans we saw on our televisions in the 1960s. Another was 'Put a tiger in your tank'. Esso Golden, Mixture and Extra were the brands sold at the Westonia Garage on Wellingborough Road. There was once a time when motorists pulled up to the old hand cranked pumps and stayed in their cars. An attendant appeared, cleaned the windscreen and dispensed the petrol. He even offered to check under the bonnet on the oil and water levels. Now we have to do it all ourselves. Yet, they are still called service stations! The Westonia was one of the first of the modern style in Northampton. It was built as the Westonia All Electric Filling Station. The reconstruction was part of a model development that included a shopping complex and tennis courts. The station was given a tiled roof and grandly christened the Westonia All Electric Filling Station. The owner lived in the upper storey of the garage, right above the job. In our picture the garage is undergoing reconstruction for the Motobaldet empire. Those were the days of relatively cheap motoring. It was not until the 1970s, when the Arab nations and the Organisation of Oil Exporting Countries (OPEC) realised their power, that motorists were made to feel they were being held to ransom. Government taxes added further burdens to the overstretched motorist. Fuel protests in the autumn of 2000 made the government aware of the weight of public feeling, but little was done to ease the financial pain felt by business and private road users.

Below: Just one glance at the faces of this pair lets you know that we are looking at a couple of real characters. Moore Marriott and Graham Moffat starred in a number of comic films. Off screen these local lads could be found in responsible positions in the community. Marriott lived at Everdon and was a councillor in Daventry. Moffat ran a pub in Braybrooke. As actors they were destined for comedy roles. Their sense of the ridiculous hardly suited them to parts in Shakespearean tragedy. Marriott and Moffat teamed up several times with the outstanding British comedy actor Will Hay. One of their best remembered performances came in 'Oh Mr Porter'. The title was inspired by one of Marie Lloyd's top music hall numbers. The 1937 film became a cinema classic. The story line, of a stationmaster in Ireland catching gunrunners disguised as ghosts, was a little thin. But, the performances of the three comedians lifted it onto another plane. The gags and one liners had the audience rolling in the aisle. Even the critics loved it. Hay, Marriott and Moffat were all given special mention in 'Halliwell's Film Guide'. That put them on a par with John Barrymore and Robert Montgomery who were given similar praise for their work in other films released that year. Britain has produced a series of comic and character actors down the years. Moore Marriott and Graham Moffat are included in that list.

Bottom: This is not a rehearsal for the old TV game show 'Three, two, one'. The 'dusty bins' in the foreground are the real thing. The group of dustmen were at the West Bridge depot during a strike in the early 1960s. This was a period of near full employment. Britain had come out of the more austere times of the 1950s and the economy was booming again. Workers had more power as there were fewer in the queue to replace them. They flexed their industrial muscle in the search for better wages and working conditions. People used to joke that in the springtime, when the daffodils came out, the dockers came out in sympathy. When the Labour government came to power in 1964 the working class felt it had an ally. Strikes bedevilled successive governments for the next 15 years as the unions fought battles with authority. These led to the three day week and the winter of discontent in the 1970s. It was not until the Thatcher years of the 1980s that

union power was curbed. In this photograph the dustmen look determined about their cause. Note the hairstyles and dress sense of the time. Thin was the byword. Slim Jim ties and drainpipe trousers, popular in the late 1950s, continued to be worn into the following decade. Men's shoes were often pointed, in a winkle-picker style. The young man to the left sports his hair in a quif, reminiscent of the American rock and roll singer, Gene Vincent.

Fuelling their own achievements

The clean forecourt of Westbridge Motors, a few hundred yards from the town's railway station in St James Road, is a familiar sight to Northampton residents and has served them and many who have passed through the town, for over sixty years; as well as selling petrol it also provided car repair services from the large workshop at the rear. It was founded by John Brocklehurst, the father of the of present day owners Robert and Nick, and his brother Cecil in 1937.

On the outbreak of hostilities in 1939, the garage was closed and designated as an emergency mortuary to be used should Northampton experience large-scale air raids. After the war, when things began to return to normal, the garage reopened, first selling 'pool' petrol, but shortly many old and well-remembered names appeared on the pumps, including 'Power', 'National Benzol', 'Shellmex' and 'BP'. The business expanded its scope of operations when John's brother-in-law, Geoff Pakes, joined in 1946 and started the Westbridge Private Hire and Taxi Service, operating with two Humber Snipes. It was his custom to sleep on the premises and this was the start of the Westbridge commitment to 24-hour service which has been a feature of the firm ever since.

The years between the end of the second world war and the 1960s saw the car change from being a luxury means of transport for the rich and famous only to an everyday necessity for many - a trend which continues today. Two-car households are common-place and four-car households not so rare nowadays so the Westbridge line of business was one in which the opportunities were extensive and consumer expectations steadily increasing.

Above: Company founder John Brocklehurst.
Below: Filling a car in post-war austerity, 1947.

In 1962, Robert Brocklehurst joined the company as an engineering apprentice, later taking responsibility for all engineering matters and, continuing the family involvement, he was joined by his brother Nick two years later who took on responsibility for the parts department and increasingly for the retail side of things, which included the major growth area of the forecourt.

When the M1 motorway was opened, the Westbridge 24-hour Breakdown and Recovery Service was launched to cater for the problems encountered by motorists who found that their cars were not designed to travel at sustained high speeds. This

Top: Westbridge Motors circa 1949/50. **Above:** *An aerial view of the site in 1947.*

proved to be a highly successful development in the business, and today Westbridge are agents for a number of the major breakdown recovery services. John Brocklehurst went into semi-retirement in 1972 and though he and his wife Evelyn remained shareholders and retained a keen interest in the company's fortunes, the day-to-day running of the company fell to their sons, Robert and Nick.

The early 1970s saw the younger generation seize great opportunities to carry the business forward. One such opening was when the eastern adjacent site came up for sale. This was purchased and it meant that the position of the garage became much more prominent and visible to the general public. This led to the redesign of the Shell forecourt which came in 1973 and incorporated the then new concept of self-service and shop facilities as well as improving access for traffic on the busy St James Road. This forward-looking approach has continued over the years and has led to the introduction of the Westbridge Charge Card which is valued by many for the speedy way it enables transactions to go through.

Along with the newly acquired land came a four-storey bonded warehouse. A major distiller approached the brothers asking whether they would be prepared to continue to offer the facility to provide warehousing facilities for it, and this further opportunity to expand and diversify was seized. Geoff Pakes set about acquiring the necessary license from Customs and Excise and learning about this specialised trade. Though they went into it on a trial basis and found it hard going at first it became a thriving concern. It couldn't operate without the computerised system which allows calculations of the precise excise duty payable - this is a complicated process which has to take into account all relevant UK and European legislation. During the national lorry drivers' strike in 1977 the bonded store brought into use its own transport to distribute whisky to

the distillers' clients customers in East Anglia. There were so many compliments on their speed and efficiency that they were asked to continue the service, which they were very pleased to do.

With this increased activity it became apparent, especially with the introduction of VAT, that it was necessary to recruit the services of a person responsible for the administration of the office procedures. In 1975 the company was fortunate in obtaining the services of Alan Wilson who previously worked for a local firm of accountants, to take over the day-to-day administration and oversight of the company's ever-increasing paper work and legal requirements. Alan was appointed Director in 1977.

Another significant development took place soon after Bernard Smith joined the company as a taxi controller. He realised that second hand mechanically tested parts on an 'off-the-shelf' basis would prove to be a valuable service, not only to customers, but also to insurance

companies who had badly damaged cars to dispose of. So Westbridge Motors became vehicle dismantlers, employing a team of professionals to strip parts from second-hand cars for steam cleaning and mechanical testing before being sold at one-third of the new part price. Their cars were brought in by their own recovery service - an ideal way of solving the insurance companies' problem of disposing of badly damaged vehicles and at the same time re-using the undamaged parts, providing a useful service to the public.

A talking point among many Northampton residents and a familiar sight to Westbridge customers was the 'half a car' which was created as a promotional idea and also shown at local carnivals.

More space was created by the acquisition in 1984 of three-quarters of an acre to the west of the Westbridge premises, and the Used Car Parts Department and the Breakdown Service was relocated there.

However in 1992 due to changes in insurance companies policies the used car parts business was sold to a larger operator, Auto Spares and Salvage of Rushden, and the building used for the expansion of the breakdown department with the balance converted into small workshop units. On the occasion of Geoff Pakes' retirement in 1983, Bernard Smith was appointed director with responsibility for the bonded warehouse and distribution side of the business.

In 1987 the bond again increased in size and the firm leased an additional 20,000 square feet of warehouse space and gained a major new contract in distribution

Top: *The firm's half-car used to promote the Westbridge Spare Parts centre.*
Left: *Robert and Nick Brocklehurst.*

car care and a wide range of food to include hot and cold snacks, sandwiches and ready meals. This was added to in 2000 when a licence was obtained to sell alcohol and spirits, wines and beers are now available. They have also benefited from having parking in front of of the store making it easier for customers to shop, especially for those heavy items such as coal and gas.

using Tautliner Scania 16 tonne vehicles designed to facilitate the needs of the operation.
However with the changing market place and EEC regulations the Bond closed in 1990.

In the 1980s the company took on the licences of three shell sites, namely Cattlemarket Filling Station, Paulersbury Self Serve and finally, in 1986, a new forecourt concept by Shell called Travellers Check on the A508 at Wootton, a site opened by Noel Edmunds, and operated until 1997.

The Company celebrated its 50th anniversary by having a stall at the Northampton Show in 1987 at which they showed some of the facets of their organisation and, among other things, held a balloon race - all profits from which went to the hospital CAT Scanner appeal. At Easter 1998 the site was part of the Northampton flood and was under three feet of water but still managed to keep trading throughout the difficult period.

With the knowledge gained in operating the Shell new concept site and following the acquisition of half an acre of land from the adjoining plot of land owned by Travis Perkins, a major redevelopment of the site started in August 1998 to build a modern forecourt with the latest technology together with a 2,000 square foot convenience store. Nick's son Karl joined the company to manage the new facility which opened in December 1998 and was shortly joined by his sister Annabel. The facility continues the Westbridge commitment to 24-hour service. The store offers a large selection of convenience goods including confectionery, soft drinks,

When the redevelopment was carried out Karl's vision for the future proposed the inclusion of a new type of auto fuel, LPG (Autogas), and it was decided to include a pump on the new forecourt, the first one to be included on a BP forecourt in England. With the increasing interest in this low-cost environmentally-friendly fuel the company now carries out conversions in its workshop.

A new conveyor car wash is due to open in April 2001, the first of its type in Northampton.

During the many changing faces of Westbridge Motors it would not have been possible for the family business to have grown to its present size and appearance without the full support and dedicated commitment given by Robert's wife Heather and Nick's wife Erika, both at home and at work.

Westbridge will undoubtedly continue to respond to changing customer needs and develop further business opportunities in the future, continuing a fine tradition already well established.

Top left: *The interior of Westbridge Motors shop.* ***Below:*** *The state-of-the-art petrol forecourt as seen today.*

Pole position

Before long it will be half a century since Mike Costin and Keith Duckworth decided to go into partnership together, combining their surnames and talents to create what was to become famed as Cosworth. Despite the two founders having now retired, the legendary name of Cosworth still remains respected throughout the world, for the design and precision engineering of high-performance race, rally and road engines.

Since Mike and Keith's retirement the company has had more than one owner and was sold most recently in 1998, splitting 'Cosworth Technology' from the more glamourous half of the business, 'Cosworth Racing'. Now owned by Ford Motor Company, Cosworth Racing remains at St James Mill Road in Northampton.

Founded in 1959, Cosworth first operated from premises at Edmonton. According to Keith Duckworth the pair of them thought it must be possible to make an 'interesting living messing about with racing cars and engines'. Neither he nor Mike Costin had anything particularly grand in mind, certainly neither of them sought nor envisaged the world-wide reputation they would eventually acquire.

In their first year, turnover amounted to just £3,666 and the business made a loss. By 1963 however when the business moved to Northampton turnover had reached almost £100,000 and Cosworth would never look back. Neither of the two partners had ever been to Northampton but deciding that it was an ideal location in the heart of the motorsport industry, a new

factory was built for £8,000. It was a wise move. The world's motor industry would come beating a path to Cosworth's doors in ever increasing numbers.

On the Motorsport World Stage, Cosworth Racing engines are currently used in all major race and rally categories including F1, CART and WRC. Committed to the cause of engineering excellence, its innovation in the design of engine technology has revolutionised modern powerplant engineering. The continuous quest for engineering ultimates has seen Cosworth keep its place not only at the forefront of the grid but also in the field of research, development and production.

Racing operations are housed on three sites; two in the UK and one in the US, employing over 700 people, each one possessing the specialist skills required to maintain Cosworth's unrivalled pedigree.

Above left: Keith Duckworth and Mike Costin, company founders. Below: Cosworth was built up in the late 1960s by four directors, left to right: Bill Brown, Keith Duckworth, Mike Costin and Ben Rood. Bottom: Victory first time out. Jim Clark drove the Ford DFV-engined Lotus 49 to victory in it's maiden race, the Dutch F1 Grand Prix in June 1967.

Teaching excellence in historic surroundings

The Red Lady and the Blue Lady, both in love with the same man; the lost village; the unearthly White Lady who circles the lake; the mysterious tale of the white peacock - stories of ghosts, mysteries and legends from the ancient past are part of the folklore of Quinton House School, formerly Upton Hall School. And what could be more understandable for an establishment whose own records are linked with a building whose history can be traced back to medieval times?

Ghosts and spirits, however, play little part in the day-to-day life of Quinton House in the third millennium, and if things go bump in the night the reason is likely to have more to do with the high spirits of children rather than the spirits of the long departed!

The complete history of Upton Hall is now lost in the mists of time. The site was occupied from the earliest times and there was once a Saxon weaving shed to the west of the church. A mill is mentioned in the Domesday Book but the survey does not mention a hall. What is certain is that the Fitzsewin family built a manor house on the site in medieval times and parts of that 'Great Hall' remain incorporated into the fabric of the present school building some of whose timbers have been dated, using tree rings, to 1507. The building was however extensively rebuilt in the 17th century and in the later Georgian period.

The school's own history goes back to 1946, when the three Misses Teape, one of whom became the first headmistress, leased the rather run-down Upton Hall and opened a school on the premises, where well brought-up children - many of them the children of servicemen - could learn to sing, dance, play the piano and gain a basic education. Before the school opened, Upton Hall, which then belonged to Sir Thomas White's Charity Trust, had fallen into a state of disrepair and was almost hidden from view among the badly overgrown grounds and driveway. The nearby woodland had expanded and spread into the grounds, and self-set elder and sycamore trees had crept relentlessly towards the hall. Few

Above: The memorial to Jane Harrington née Samwell in Milton Church. Below: South view of Upton Hall as it was in the last century.

were only admitted up to the age of ten. The physical and spiritual health of pupils featured high on Miss Teape's list of priorities. Games, including tennis, cricket, hockey, netball and rounders in addition to swimming, were organised every day, and the school doctor attended regularly. The prospectus described the diet as 'liberal, varied and very nourishing' and the children's meals benefited from the vegetables, fresh fruit and salads that were grown in the school's own four acres of kitchen garden and orchard.

people at that time were interested in renovating such large properties and their adjoining acres of land; the second world war had recently ended and post-war prosperity in Britain was still a long way off.

By the summer of 1947 however Upton Hall School was ready to take its very first pupils: two young girls. With honour, discipline and diligence as its principles, the school officially opened in the autumn, with seven boarders and around the same number of day girls. Boarders were taken from the age of five. Both girls and boys were accepted by the school, with a five percent reduction for sisters and brothers attending at the same time, though boys

Above left: *The Hudson family were the last private owners of Upton Hall from 1893 - 1946.*
Above right: *The church of St Michael was endowed by families at the hall. It is now looked after and used by Quinton House School.*

The children attended St Michael's, the charming little Norman church nearby, every Sunday and were prepared for confirmation if their parents wished it.

Miss Teape retired in 1962, and Upton Hall School was taken over by Mr and Mrs MacDonald. The sixties saw a nationwide rebellion among young people, who began to demand freedom from authority and control. A strict discipline was retained, however, at Upton Hall. Senior girls were allowed to go shopping in Northampton on Saturdays only, and then only with the consent of their parents. And woe betide any of the girls who were seen speaking to a boy! The happiness of the pupils, however, was of great importance, and 'old girls' who revisited the school recently assured the present staff that they had thoroughly enjoyed their school life.

Quinton House came into being after the early death of Mrs MacDonald, when Miss Madden took over as head teacher in September 1963 and renamed the school.

Top: *The exterior of the school.*
Below: *Stucco work in the ballroom done by Bugatti & Artari in 1737 portrays the Greek god Mercury - the messenger.*
Left: *The 14th Century timbered roof.*

Boarders were taken from the age of six to sixteen and Miss Madden set out to create a homely atmosphere for the children.

Another policy was that of fostering the key attributes of personal tidiness, grooming and good manners. At the end of every day each child had to have a wash and brush up and be checked for tidiness by the teacher before leaving for home. Most classes had their own bathroom, and each child's hair brush, comb and towel were laid out there on individual trays.

Though the children were expected to be well mannered, this did not check their high spirits - or stop the odd childish prank such as piling books on top of a door ready to fall on the head of the first member of staff to walk through it!

Despite the range of sporting activities offered to the pupils of Quinton House the equipment and facilities were in fact rather limited. Running took place along the main driveway, netball was played on a small gravelled play area (disastrous to the knees of any child who happened to fall!) and tennis was relegated to an area near the lake. An interesting comment from a former member of staff was that the students of ballet, of which the school had many at the time, were not required to play hockey in case the dancers' legs were injured.

In 1976 Mr and Mrs Hoskison took over from Miss Madden and decided to admit senior boys for the first time. A new air of adventure, danger and enthusiasm suddenly hit the school, and the staff and pupils alike

*Top: Junior School pupils in their library. **Above right:** A group of Sixth Formers.*

had to accustom themselves to their presence which brought a refreshingly different atmosphere to the school. Sporting facilities were enhanced by the addition of new hard surface tennis courts.

The Borough Council took over the administration of Upton Hall in 1986, when the Northampton Development Corporation was wound up. It was decided that the buildings should be re-roofed, and the old tiles were accordingly removed. Disaster struck during the night, when an unexpected storm brought a deluge that soaked desks, carpets, cloakrooms, blackboards and books.

Exams were imminent and work had to go on; sodden carpets were rolled up and carried away, text books were dried out, and the children did their best to concentrate on lessons while workmen clambered about overhead, disturbing the wet plaster that fell from the ceilings on to their work. Staff soldiered on with damp blackboards and soggy pieces of chalk. In 1988 Mr and Mrs Griffiths took charge of the school. It was growing swiftly at the time, and in response to the expansion a number of rearrangements were made at Quinton House; senior students were placed in the Hall itself, while the junior school was moved to the Lindens, an old stable block which had been brought into use. The changes allowed a new nursery unit to be developed, and quarters suitable for such young children were constructed.

The following year saw the formation of the Parents' Association, and a very first Christmas Ball was organised by two of the parents. Since then the Association has gone from strength to strength, organising fetes, 5th November bonfire celebrations, fathers v school cricket matches and open days. Though fund raising is not its primary concern, the Association has provided much-needed drama equipment and is responsible for the newly-extended sports pavilion. Sport has always taken an important place in the school curriculum, and in 1990 it was decided to lay a new football pitch in what had been the old walled garden. An overgrown area of thistles and weeds, the site seemed to be an ideal choice. What could be simpler? Clear it and level the ground.... Things

turned out to be far more complicated than that, however. It appeared that the Saxons had at one time built a pottery there, and as the walled garden contained a site of historical importance it was not possible to level the ground completely. The sports pitch was built, though with a significant gradient that was to make itself

*Left, **both pictures:*** *Netball and cricket are popular parts of the sporting curriculum.*
Below: *Some of the Nursery/Pre-School pupils.*

universities are encouraged. One of the school's most exciting events is its bi-annual Sixth Form conference when students gather for a full day at a high class conference centre for a course based on social skills which culminates in a full evening dress formal dinner.

The basic principles on which Quinton House School was founded still hold good. Hard work, discipline and good manners are as important today as ever, though more freedom of expression is

felt among those teams who had to play uphill!

By 1992 Mr and Mrs Griffiths felt that if the school was to develop as they wanted, they needed to add a Sixth Form in order to offer their students more advanced studies. The new facility added a further dimension to the school - not all of it desirable, such as loud music echoing from the Sixth Form Common Room! In time, the first of the sixth formers graduated and went on to university life or to further professional training within their field of employment.

The Sixth Form has developed each year and new subjects have been added to the curriculum and an extensive social programme evolved. Staff are aware that in a small Sixth Form outlooks can become very insular and therefore students must understand what is happening beyond the school walls. Consequently visits to conferences, interaction with foreign students in Europe and America and links with colleges and

encouraged. A family atmosphere is still fostered within the school, and the staff firmly believe in valuing each pupil as an individual. Personal integrity and care and compassion for others are cultivated, and this is reflected in the school's commitment to a wide variety of charitable works. Each House at the Hall chooses a charity to support each year, including such diverse areas as riding for the disabled, sponsoring animals at Twycross Zoo, leukaemia in children, the Higgins Fund for AIDS, Northampton Soup Kitchen, Children in Need, Red Nose Day, research into breast cancer and many more. The junior school works just as hard for similar charities. They have raised money to provide alarms to prevent cot deaths, provided a guide dog for a blind person and helped Children in Need. The combined efforts

Above left: *Information Technology plays an important part in the life of the school.*
Below: *The whole school pictured in 2000.*

throughout Quinton House School raises between £3,000 and £4,000 each year.

A wide curriculum is offered at Quinton House, and science, technology and information technology feature highly on the school's timetable. Computing facilities are available to all the pupils, and a specialist information technology unit offers the opportunity to keep abreast of today's developments. History and geography, music, science, elocution and dancing, art and craft all form part of the timetable. Religious Education is based on Christian teaching but tolerance and understanding of other faiths is promoted among the children from an early age. Languages include French and German - in fact French is taught from the age of seven and German from the age of nine..

The Millennium year did not go by unnoticed. All the pupils received a cut glass paperweight engraved with letters 'QHS celebrates the year 2000'. The school also put on a wonderful musical show with song and dance, illustrating the previous 2000 years, and a grand all-day party when all the pupils and staff dressed as period characters. It didn't look at all out of place in the school's lovely setting to see Edwardian ladies complete with parasols strolling in the gardens, or Henry VIII and one of his six queens sauntering down the drive.

But there was also sadness. In July 2000 Gerald Griffiths retired after 40 years of teaching and although he had a really good send off it was an emotional time for all. The Deputy Headmaster Charles Oliver took over the headship in September 2000.

Although surrounded by history Quinton House School does not live in the past. It has the latest technological equipment and students enjoy access to the internet and e-mail to make friendships with children in other parts of the world especially in Canada, the USA and in Africa where pupils can work with other children via e-mail.

Today Headmaster Charles Oliver and his staff can be justifiably proud of the students who leave Quinton House School as confident, well-balanced young men and women - and their commitment is to take the school forward into the new millennium with continued dedication to the highest possible standards.

Above: Retiring Headmaster, Mr Griffiths, left, with the new Headmaster Mr Oliver, Head-boy, Nicholas Harding and Head-girl, Pretti Patel, July 2000.

Stepping out in style

The world-famous footwear manufacturers Crockett & Jones was founded in 1879 by Charles Jones and his brother-in-law James Crockett. Neither of them had any capital and in order to set up in business they each applied for a grant of £100 to the Sir James Thomas White Trust, a famous endowment founded in the 16th century by Sir Thomas (who later went on to become the Lord Mayor of London) with the purpose of encouraging young men to go into business in the City of Coventry.

At this time footwear factories were small but acted as an important link between the hand-made shoemakers who worked from home and the retailers. The leather was cut in factories and the shoemaker collected it and the other components from there. Even as late as 1900 the price of a pair of shoes made in this way was six shillings (30p).

An important factor in the firm's success was the way they integrated machinery and the human skills in the production of their high-quality footwear - in fact the company had the reputation for making some of the best machine made shoes available. The expertise in the company enabled them to respond to the demanding assignment of

supplying the footwear for two of Shackleton's Polar expeditions.

In 1924 the Duke of York, later King George VI paid a visit to the factory, an event which gave them considerable publicity in the national as well as local press. A national advertising campaign organised in 1927 led to an increased demand for Crockett & Jones shoes and in 1935 a second wing was added to the factory in Perry Street. This factory is itself of special interest for when it was originally built in 1910 it was believed to be the first steel structure building in Northampton and provides workers with very good working conditions with superb natural lighting and ventilation to this day.

James Crockett was knighted in 1921 for his services to the town of Northampton and the footwear industry - his example of community and industrial service has been followed by succeeding generations of company executives.

From the early part of the 20th century, the company was involved in exporting. In those days, exports were mainly to the dominion countries plus the USA. After the second world war the world markets changed,

Top left: Sir James Crockett. ***Top right:*** *Charles Jones.* ***Above:*** *A selection of gentlemen's footwear from the early 1900s.* ***Right:*** *A display panel from the early part of the 20th century.*

and the company's emphasis in exporting was switched to the USA, Japan and Europe. Today more than 40 per cent of their shoes are sold to European Community countries.

The company is keen to preserve the traditional skills for the production of shoes but is always happy to introduce modern production methods provided that high standards of quality are not compromised. Each pair of shoes takes up to eight weeks to produce using the traditional Goodyear welted process which produces shoes of exceptional strength comfort and durability. The present Managing Director is the fourth generation of the Jones family to be managing the business and the company ethos remains very much what it was when originally founded, though nowadays the business is much more complex and wide-ranging than it was in 1879.

Each week the Crockett & Jones output is in the region of 2,000 pairs of shoes and between four and five hundred styles are in production at any one time.

Around 75 per cent of output goes for export much of it to the world's most stylish centres such as Tokyo, Milan, Paris and New York - and, of course,- London. In 1990 the company was awarded The Queen's Award for Export. In 1997 the company opened its own flagship shop in Jermyn Street which has long been where the most elegant and affluent purchase their shirts and shoes. It mainly caters for the men's market but still produces a women's range of shoes. In 1998 a shop was opened in Paris and in 1999 a second shop in London.

The firm has doubled its staff in the last twenty years but training a highly-skilled workforce is not something that can happen overnight and making some of the world's finest footwear is not a job that can be rushed. Crockett & Jones is committed to providing the discerning customer with its high quality products and will continue to so in the future.

Top: *A view of the closing room at the Perry Street factory in the 1960s.*
Above left: *An advertisement from the first half of the 20th century.*
Right: *Richard Jones, Company Chairman since 1979.*

A *down-to-earth family*

'Keeping it in the family' has often proved a recipe for success in business and this is being demonstrated by two generations of Northampton business men who are continuing a long tradition of family businesses run by the Darby family. Edwin Arthur James Darby is perpetuating a line of business established by his father, also Edwin, who was in business with his brother AW Darby who at their peak ran in the region of 80 lorries.

Leaving St Lawrence College at the age of sixteen, Edwin Junior served five years apprenticeship at British Timken as a machinery and tool fitter. He spent many an evening servicing his father's lorries. At the age of 21 he was conscripted into the RAF where he was trained in general engineering. After 18 months based in Scampton, Lincolnshire, he returned to British Timken for a short time before joining the family business which was then known as Acme Building Co. which ran together with BSC which were both associate companies of AW Darby Transport. The plant hire was incorporated in 1966 and ran for about five years as BSC Plant Hire.

There were at this time no less than 18 members of the Darby family involved in the business and Edwin felt there was scope for him to branch out on his own and so it was that in 1969 E & A Plant Services came into existence. with Mrs Anne Darby as Company Secretary.

Edwin rented premises at Ransome Road, Far Cotton to begin with. In the very early days, during his first year of trading, he worked alone but later was able to employ a fitter and an office assistant. These three members of staff continued to work together for the next three years when they were joined by a plant

Above: *Company founder Edwin AJ Darby.*
Below: *A 1930s Albion flat truck, part of AW Darby's haulage fleet.*

Above: Edwin AJ Darby talking to a Benford engineer and sales representative, 1969.

lorry driver who is still an active and valued employee of the firm.

At this time the company supplied compressors, drills, rammers, signs and the occasional JCB for 15 gangs for Murphy's gas division covering two contracts in Northamptonshire for projects in Corby, Kettering and Northampton town for the cut-offs and redevelopment of terraced houses. During the 1970s and early 1980s they won a contract from British Rail to serve track maintenance crews with two digger machines with operators on weekend repair work from midnight Saturday to noon Sunday on the Bletchley to Rugby line lifting rail tracks and digging land drains.

The firm has been involved in supplying equipment to four of the most prestigious contracts to be undertaken in Northampton in recent times. In the mid-1970s they supplied compressors and tools for the demolition of the old Electric Power Station furnace chimneys in Nunn Mills Road. The compressors were run with shoulder guns to complete the work from the top of the inside by hand. The work was completed in six weeks, well ahead of schedule. They also supplied diggers and operators for over 14 months together with other non-operated plant when the £9million extension to the Avon Cosmetics premises was undertaken in the early 1980s. Tools were also supplied to facilitate the work on the Derngate Theatre, Guildhall Road, Northampton. Diggers with operators and a full plant hire service was given over a two year period to Penman builders for the redevelopment of Notre Dame School.

During the 1980s it was E & A Plant which supplied mixers and dumpers and small tools for Bacal Contracting for the new Tesco warehouse in Milton Keynes, a new school in Clapham Road, Bedford, Lodge Farm, Northampton and Bacal's new office block and numerous housing sites.

They also served Kottler and Heron during this period of time until both companies ceased trading. The 1980s also saw the firm supply the local Bartram Construction which had won a contract for road, sewers and housing for a period of two years with dumpers, rollers and small tools on three sites in North London. Also at this time D & L Civil Engineering hired their machines with

operators, running five machines at any one time working on contracts at Bletchley, Aylesbury, Bedford and Milton Keynes.

A great strength of the firm has always been its ability to offer friendly service backed up by a team which is fully trained in their particular areas of work. The company is still very much a family concern and in the same way that Edwin carried on a line of business in which his father was involved, so it is that Edwin's youngest son, John, is now spearheading the current day-to-day operation of E & A Plant, drawing on the experience and advice of Edwin, and being ably assisted by his wife Vicki. John joined the firm when he had completed his training at CITB and joined the business as an enthusiastic digger driver. His sister Lisa is also

*Top left: Gerry Pettit and Edwin Darby celebrating more than 100,000 plant deliveries and collections in over 25 years service. **Right:** Edwin Darby with his son John. **Below:** Some of the fleet at Monarch Road, 1998.*

presently involved in the firm. The business also benefited from the input of the eldest Darby son, Edwin Junior during the 1980s.

It was during that time, 1984 to be precise, that the firm moved to its present premises in Monarch Road, Kingsthorpe Hollow, Northampton. Edwin had encountered considerable difficulty over the years finding a suitable location which also had the necessary permission to site his vehicles and machinery, but the Monarch Road site fitted the bill and the company has operated from there ever since.

Over the years the trend has been towards gradual expansion up to the present time when a truly comprehensive range of equipment is on offer. Tipper lorries, excavators, dumpers, rollers, compressors, bowsers, mixers, pumps, generators, vibrators, floor surface equipment such as floor saws, floor planers and grinders, a

road brush, industrial vacuum cleaners, saw benches, post hole borers, heaters, spray equipment, saws, a site safe, rotavator, rotary mower, seed spreader and strimmer in addition to ladders and a wide range of building tools and road working equipment are all available from E & A Plant today.

Such a range was not built up overnight and the scope of service offered has gradually built up over the years. One significant development came in 1980 when the firm started to offer skip hire facilities. There are now two skip lorries operating, servicing over 100 skips. In addition to hiring their extensive range of equipment, E & A also offer sales and repair services.

Nowadays the customer base changes more rapidly as contracts are now only short term but the E & A service is offered to over 130 companies at any one time including Wright & Smith, M J Green Builders, Shackleton Construction Ltd, Turner Builders, C Smith Developments, M C Midlands, Jon Par and others, many of whom have been trading with them for over twenty years.

With ever changing demands on the construction industry the firm continually strives to meet the demands of all its customers. Recent innovations have included the 26T Grab Lorry to include the supply of aggregates, ballast and sand and after many years of continued membership of the Construction Plant Association they are now members of The Road Haulage Association.

Above right: *Taking delivery of three CAT 428 in 1998.* ***Left:*** *A 17 tonne skip lorry.* ***Below:*** *The 26T Grab Lorry.*

A blueprint for progress

Who was the first architect? If not quite the oldest profession then architecture can surely claim to be second. Its unique blend of art and science can trace its origins back to the builders of the Pyramids of ancient Egypt where the set-square and dividers first became the badge of the profession some four thousand years or more ago.

In the millennia which have passed since the sun first shone on the wonders of the ancient world the profession of architecture has never looked back. The skill and expertise of its practitioners becoming evermore sophisticated whilst being responsible for the ever changing face of our towns and cities.

The Northampton firm of architects Peter Haddon and Partners - PHP - was, unsurprisingly, founded by one man, Peter Haddon. Today the small firm he founded is Northampton's largest architectural practice, based in The Old Rectory at Milton Malsor and now enjoys an annual fee turnover in excess of one million pounds.

Prior to starting his own architectural firm Peter Haddon had worked as a partner with Marsham, Warren & Taylor but in 1965 he determined to branch out on his own. The new venture started life from two offices above St John Ambulance in Northampton's York Road where the fledgling firm would be based for the following six years.

Six months after starting out Peter Haddon was joined by Leslie G Kingston who had spent his post graduate year working on designs for a British School of Film and Television.

Unlike today, where computer graphics are the norm, the business was then conducted entirely using those traditional architects' drawing materials - mapping pens and tracing paper pinned onto drawing boards to produce clients' blueprints.

Clients were attracted in significant numbers and by 1971 the firm moved to 8 Albion Place where the whole of the three storey building was occupied.

The practice continued to grow steadily and the move to Milton Malsor was made in 1976 by which time more space was again needed. The village was chosen because of its proximity to Junction 15 of the motorway. Since then the property has been extended and the practice has taken over the adjoining cottage. In the late 1980s the two staff had grown to 26 including five principal partners and three associate partners. By then the firm was winning prestigious contacts such as that to design and supervise the new multi-million pound offices for the Meat and Livestock Commission in Milton Keynes.

Above: Peter Haddon who founded the practice in 1965. Below: The Old Rectory at Milton Malsor, now home to Peter Haddon and Partners.

What has been the secret of PHP's continuous growth? The answers are varied: but include the quality of its designs coupled with innovation backed by the firm's design expertise, project management skills and excellent client service. And no doubt ensuring that buildings of quality are constructed on time and on budget have helped continuously enhance the firm's reputation.

Today, as always, Peter Haddon and Partners aim to employ the best staff using state of the art equipment and to serve existing clients with the same continuing standards of excellence whilst expanding to accommodate new clients in the future.

But not all designs were for such massive projects: a few years earlier the firm had beaten 169 competitors to win the 'affordable homes' competition run by Woman magazine to design low cost homes for first time buyers. It was attention to detail which won the prize, not least ensuring that the obvious was not overlooked - where possible rooms were designed to be exactly 12 feet wide between skirtings, the identical width of a standard carpet!

Today the firm's main markets are in designing industrial and commercial buildings in addition to projects relating to the food industry. Clients have included such well known businesses and organisations as Carlsberg, George Adams & Sons, the Baker Group, NCC, the Open University, Prologis, Hampton Brook, Marriotts and Swallow Construction. Their latest success has been the winning of a prestigious European wide competition to design and project manage a £6 million office building for the Open University at Milton Keynes. Overseas the firm has been involved in food industry projects in locations as far away as Saudi Arabia, Venezuela and Singapore.

From ancient Egypt the torch of architectural skills has been passed from generation to generation. Architects of the past are responsible for our architectural heritage; today architects like PHP are now taking responsibility for the heritage that we, in turn, will bequeath to our successors.

Above, both pictures: *Two examples of the work undertaken by the firm in recent years.*
Below: *Another view of the Old Rectory.*

An engineering triumph

How do you move a bus engine easily from one side of a garage to the other? The firm of Brixworth Engineering, based at Creaton Road, Brixworth and founded in 1962 by two partners Dick Walker and his nephew Basil Lockwood, eventually found the perfect solution to that difficult problem. A suitable building was not immediately available in 1962 so an acre of land was leased on the site of demolished brickworks owned by the London Brick Company. An obsolete prefabricated concrete building 30ft by 80ft was bought for £50 - the purchasers to do the dismantling. The dismantling proved difficult, only the roof, purlings and columns survived the process. The building had to be virtually rebuilt by the firm's two founders with no building experience between them. The building is still on the present site however, and in use to this day.

In the early days Dick attended to the engineering side of the business. Basil took care of the administration and transport as well as assisting with warehousing.

An additional prefabricated building was erected in 1964 and a new purpose-built machine shop in 1969 along with an office block in 1970 and a welding shop in 1972. The machine shop was in turn extended when a new welding shop was built and a new machine shop and office block built in 1994. Things did not always go smoothly however: the recession of 1988 left the firm badly hit and economies needed to be made, not least sub-letting part of the machine shop.

Main customers are engine and gearbox manufacturers and engine service

companies - especially in the Middle East -, and aircraft manufacturers and other users of special purpose manipulators for assembly and welding requirements. Customers include the Cumming Engine Company, Mercedes Benz, Ford, Shorts Aircraft, Cosworth, Jaguar and McLaren.

The firm's main source of its success is in producing mobile engine stands which are used to rotate heavy

Above right: *Young Dick in the early days of the company.*
Right: *The first engine made by the company stands outside the original building.*

'out of balance' loads without backlash. But the firm's strength lies in the ability to design special products to customers' specification and to respond rapidly to those requests. The firm is proud of its reputation for producing a reliable first class product. The proof of that is amply demonstrated by the fact that the first engine stand it delivered in 1966 is still giving good service.

According to company history, whilst demonstrating the engine stand's ability to to hold a bus engine at the Chiswick works of London Transport in 1968, to a small group of foremen and managers, a large aggressive shop convener came out with the comment "what's this load of bleeding rubbish?". Dick, the salesman, who was a turner, miller, sweeper up and also the boss, left both the machine and the meeting with his tail between his legs and in a state of complete depression. Within a week however the large aggressive shop convener had been transformed into a friendly helpful fitter who was now insisting that the whole engineering department (which handled 60 engines a week) should be equipped with the wonderful new 'Benco' stand.

And if it was good enough for London Transport it was good enough for others. Soon orders followed from Ford, Leyland and most importantly other bus repair garages in the UK.

Not everything was quite so successful however: an enquirer from the Deutz Engine Company asked 'What's the largest engine you can accommodate?' 'Anything up to five tonnes' came the proud reply: sadly Deutz made marine engines weighing up to 50 tonnes. (Today the firm's maximum is 20 tonnes).

Perhaps the company's underlying philosophy has helped it. The business is committed to maintaining its hard won reputation and to ensuring that all its workforce gains benefits from its continued success. In these days of intense production methods the firm continues to offer individual attention to individual requirements. And arguably the firm's greatest secret is in applying team strength to individual requirements in order to achieve the most efficient and competitive methods of production.

Basil left in 1986 and his responsibilities were taken on by Daphne Walker who sadly passed away in 1992. Dick retired in 2000 and the company is now controlled by their children Martyn Walker and Susan Muir.

In the future, despite competition from Sweden and the USA, the firm plans to extend its design and manufacturing facilities to cover a complete range of special purpose mechanical handling system and devices. The firm handles heavy items, not only through 360° in one plane but 90° in the other, controlled by electrical, hydraulic and pneumatic devices as required by the customers.

A very well respected and old established Northampton company, Messrs JA Perkins, has now been incorporated in the Brixworth Engineering Co Ltd establishment.

But despite having a world beating specialist product the firm's maxim remains today, as it always has been, 'You name it we'll make it!'.

Above left: *Dick at the Automechanika Trade Fair in Germany.* ***Below:*** *Testing 976 mobile with a 2.25 tonne load outside the original building (which is still in use) and the lean-to.*

Years not minutes

'**E**ducation, education, education', was Prime Minister Tony Blair's long remembered election cry. Whether the slogan made any difference remains a matter for debate but the words may well have triggered off, in many, recollections of their own education. Were our school days the best of our lives? Again the debate must rage - if some of us have fond memories of helpful teachers and long held friendships, some of which have persisted to this day, others may recall less happy memories of bullying and teachers who made our lives miserable with lines, detentions and a clip round the ear. Whether our memories are good or bad however the one thing we all share is the simple fact that we do remember. The memory of all our school days is indelible and meeting someone from the old days inevitably brings back those memories and immediately triggers joint reminiscences. And fortunately, for most of us, our recollections are indeed happy ones.

'Fill the Unforgiving Minute' a line from Rudyard Kipling's poem 'If" is a more than fitting motto for any school. Back in 1954 it was those words which were chosen by the new headmaster Leslie A Scott for the new school placed in his charge. That new school was Moulton Secondary Modern, a school then recently completed to take pupils from a catchment area of fourteen villages.

Today Moulton is a comprehensive school for pupils aged 11 to 18 with almost 1,200 students enrolled at the beginning of the millennium, including a sixth form of 175. It currently has a staff of 67 full time and 5 part time teachers.

Moulton School's first headmaster Leslie Scott remained with the school for twenty five years until retirement in 1979. He died only in January 1999 after enjoying two decades of retirement.

The school opened its doors to pupils on 1st September 1954 and took in 339 pupils aged from 11 to 15. There were just four forms of first year students and two forms each of second and fourth

Above: *A copy of the school's magazine produced annually between 1954 and 1979.* ***Below:*** *Speech Day 1974, Leonard Cozzolino (Head Boy), Mr Scott, Mrs R Park, Mr B Carr (chief guest), Mr D Barratt, Mrs J Mahon, Susan Blewitt (Head Girl).*

and shoe industry.

Maroon blazers, the central feature of the new school uniform, would soon become a familiar sight throughout the area. (The word blazer incidentally being a reference to Saint Blaize the patron saint of woolcombers who is said to have discovered the art of wool combing). And short trousers. Whilst not compulsory shorts were still considered the norm for younger boys: when the school had opened almost every one of the younger boys wore short trousers for school, and even by 1960 fewer than a third of the new first form intake had graduated to long trousers. How times have changed! Sometime in the 1960s shorts disappeared as acceptable wear for young boys and now few if any have the chance to get their knees brown at playtime as their fathers once did.

Moulton School today is a co-educational, seven form entry, comprehensive school still drawing pupils from fourteen villages outside the borough served by primary schools in Moulton, Overstone, Sywell, Walgrave, Brixworth, Halstone, Chapel Brampton, Boughton and Pitsford. The pupil roll has increased tremendously over the years; by 1960 numbers had risen to six hundred, a figure which would inevitably rise again with those in authority by then confidently predicting that within another five years more than half those aged fifteen in the country would still be at school rather than leaving on their fifteenth birthdays as many still did. Who then would have dared to predict that continuing in education well beyond sixteen, let alone fourteen,

year pupils divided into four 'houses': Bannister, Fleming, Hillary and Whittle named after those four famous men of the period - record-breaking athlete Dr Roger Bannister, Sir Alexander Fleming the discoverer of penicillin, Sir Edmund Hillary who together with his companion Sherpa Tensing Norgay had the previous year become the first man to scale Mount Everest and lastly Sir Frank Whittle the pioneer of the jet engine. Each name was an inspiration in a separate field of endeavour whilst the school arms reflected similar virtues, quartered to show a globe, a bull's head, a cobbler's last and a pen and scroll, reminders of local Baptist Minister and Missionary William Carey who made a leather globe, whilst the scroll reflected his scholarship. The bulls head represents agriculture, a local strong point and the cobbler's last is a reminder of the area's boot

Top left: Pupils in the library in the mid 1970s.
*Above: The netball team in 1954. **Right:** A group of pupils gather before school.*

Indeed the school's examination results are amongst the best in the county of Northamptonshire .

Perhaps the school's underlying ethos summed up in its motto is best explained in a poem written by Betty Rose then a fourth year pupil in Whittle House which appeared in the very first edition of the school magazine, The Moultonian, back in 1954:

"In school we all should read and learn,
In everything should wait our turn,
In work and play should try our best,
For night's the time when we should rest,
We really know there's something in it
So let's fill the unforgiving minute."

Wise words indeed!

would become the norm for future generations? Extensions to the original building were made in 1960, 1973, 1977, 1990, 1991, 1992, 1998 and 2000. Since 1992 the school has been able to provide sports and leisure facilities for the local community via Moulton Sports Complex catering for all age groups from holiday play schemes for primary school age children to tea dances from senior citizens

In recent years the school campus has been enriched by the magnificent RIBA award winning Sixth Form Centre, a superb sports hall and community centre, a mathematics building and a refurbished science building providing eight laboratories. At the beginning of the new millennium an equally impressive structure appeared on the site with the construction of a new English and Drama centre including a mini Drama Studio as well as classrooms to accommodate English, ICT and special needs.

And do Mouton School pupils fill every unforgiving minute with hard work? They certainly manage to fill many of them: the school enjoys an excellent academic record which they work hard to maintain. Teachers are proud to be part of the school and achieve satisfaction in seeing students of all abilities attain their personal best. Pupils at the top of the ability range obtain results which compare with the best results of selective schools, a fact borne out by the numbers of university placements secured each year by those leaving the upper sixth form.

Top left: An aerial view of the school. Left: Pupils studying in the library in the 1990s. Right: Mr JN Woodhead, Headmaster. Below: Oxbridge candidates visiting Cambridge University in 1997.

Digging for knowledge

Moulton College, formerly Northamptonshire Farm Institute, is situated in the village of Moulton five miles to the north of Northampton.

The main college consists of buildings for student teaching, recreational and residential facilities along with a 440 hectare farm, equestrian centre and a commercial horticultural unit. An indoor riding school was opened in 1991 and a construction studies, computer and furniture craft workshop in 1993 whilst throughout the 1990s other buildings such as additional classrooms, offices, laboratories and workshops were added to the site. In 2000 further work studios and a sports and leisure complex were opened. New en-suite accommodation for 96 students, ten further classrooms a new garden centre and a veterinary hospital will complete the current phase of development.

Right: The 1930s Northamptonshire Farm Institute. Below: Students maintaining equipment in the 1950s.

The Institute was opened in 1921 and, with the exception of the war years when members of the Women's Land Army were trained there, has been training agricultural students ever since.

Originally the Institute comprised Home Farm and property in West Street - two detached houses and four cottages for farm staff. One of the houses was occupied by the Principal the other providing a dining room and common room for students as well as accommodation for staff. In the grounds two

wooden buildings provided bedrooms for students in addition to a lecture room and laboratory. The Institute afforded excellent facilities for the investigation of farming problems and served as an experimental station; it also offered instruction to rural teachers. Short courses were offered in agriculture,

horticulture, cheese making, poultry management and fruit bottling. A service was offered to farmers providing analysis of soils, manures, feedstuffs and milk as well as such other important problems as the purity of seeds.

By 1930 it was clear that better buildings were needed and in 1933 Mrs A S Harrison donated Red Hill Farm, Wellingborough (renamed the Thomas Harrison Farm in honour of the donor's late husband), along with £10,000 towards the building of a "new institute" which included a hostel for 40 students and further lecture rooms.

With the outbreak of war in 1939 all ordinary courses were cancelled. The first war-time course for Women's Land Army trainees began on 18th September 1939 and continued throughout the war. In all some 1,300 women received training at the Institute.

In addition to providing training for the WLA, staff were also actively involved in encouraging the work of the Women's Institute Produce Guild, the Pigs

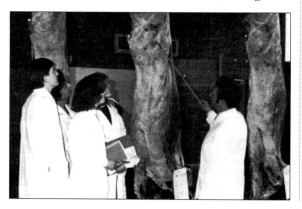

Clubs and the County Allotment Holders to increase home production of food. The famous 'Dig for Victory' slogan was taken very literally and wartime food shortages would undoubtedly have been far worse had it not been for the practical help and encouragement given by the Institute to those who struggled to add to Britain's diminishing food stocks as the German U-boats successfully sank millions of tons of shipping heading for the British Isles. Herr Hitler must have been told - the work of the Institute was not helped when in October 1941 the site was bombed by the Luftwaffe!

Normal courses at the Institute were able to resume in 1944 and it soon became clear that the amount of student accommodation would need to be increased substantially. Field House was opened in 1946 when 82 students were enrolled. The Institute increased the size of the farm again in 1945 when the lease of a Stud Farm was obtained - the 315 acres eventually being purchased in 1961.

Apart from the war years the Institute had not provided education for women; that was to change in 1952 - though the experiment ran for only two years. It would not be until 1962 that women became a permanent feature at the Institute.

The first Principal of the Institute was WA Stewart. Astonishingly he retired only in 1958 after almost 38 years of service. Under his direction the Institute had become known not only nationally but also

Above: *Students taking part in a pageant in 1955.* ***Left:*** *Students studying beef production in the 1970s.*

internationally. The Institute's reputation and profile had undoubtedly been increased immeasurably by a series of radio broadcasts by the Principal in the mid 1930s, soon followed by an exhibition at the Smithfield Show where the Institute's best mutton carcass made the highest price at the show.
In 1959 the Farm Machinery Workshop was completed on Home Farm and a lecturer in Farm Machinery appointed - a harbinger of the modern world and the increasing role which technology would begin to play in agriculture.

The 1960s would be a decade of growth for the Institute with a new teaching wing, a demonstration kitchen, staff offices and accommodation for 100 students together with a new common room and library. Additionally a bee-keeping centre, demonstration potting shed and building workshop were added to the Institute's facilities.

The Thomas Harrison Farm would be absorbed into the Wellingborough Town scheme to accommodate London overspill population. The farm had to be replaced and the 365 acre Moulton Lodge Farm adjoining the Home and Stud Farms was acquired in 1969 along with 100 further acres.

In 1966 the Institute became a College after the Pilkington Report of that year suggested that county agricultural establishments calling

themselves schools or institutes set themselves apart from technical colleges to no particular purpose. In response to changing farm structures and husbandry techniques new courses were introduced as farms became larger and more specialised whilst the number of farmers and employees fell.

Since 1992 many farm buildings have been replaced with clear span structures, the traditional Victorian buildings being converted to classrooms, offices and laboratories. The farm operates a range of enterprises each with its own manager and, whilst the farms serve an educational need they are managed commercially and perform to commercial standards.

Throughout the 1990s the College has continued to expand at an astonishing rate - from fewer than 100 full time students at the start of the decade to almost a thousand by the end whilst over four thousand part time students were being provided with tuition at the start of the new millennium.

Today, from its small beginnings, Moulton College is known throughout the country as a centre of excellence with courses of study available in a dozen subject areas. These range from the traditional subjects of agriculture, animal care and arboriculture through to modern specialities such as countryside management, rural skills, furniture making, floristry, construction and sports management completing the range of courses on offer. The College is a nationally recognised centre for conferences , seminars and short courses.

Above left: *Modern Countryside Management students.* ***Below:*** *Principal, Chris Moody presenting NVQ Level 3 certificates in Construction to Daniel Kellock and Samantha Stone in 1999.*

Generations of dignified service

In this world we can be certain of only two things as the old saying goes: death and taxes. And if death is a certainty then sooner or later we are bound to need the service of a professional undertaker. Choosing an undertaker for the delicate task of making funeral arrangements for a loved one is inevitably a sad process but one made immeasurably easier by the degree of dignity and professional skill which can only be obtained by employing an undertaking firm which has been in business for more than a century.

The well known local firm of funeral directors, SE Wilkinson & Son, was established in 1877 at premises at 30 Grove Road where the business is still to be found today; its roots can be traced back to those far off days through carefully preserved hand written ledgers containing details of the very first funerals it carried out. Back then the firm used horse drawn carriages to convey the deceased to their final resting place; how times have changed!

The firm also owns many references to both itself and the Wilkinson family which have appeared both in local literature and in the form of aged, now yellowing, newspaper clippings referring to prominent members of the family. One member of the family was Dr AG Wilkinson who served his country at the Barrack Hospital, Scutari, outside Constantinople working alongside the

renowned Florence Nightingale during the Crimean War. Dr Wilkinson became well known for his work in Northampton and much respected by the townsfolk during his life, not least for his role in delivering more than 600 of the town's babies. Following a very full and eventful life he died as late as 1923, at the advanced age of 88, passing away at his home and surgery at 28 Newland Northampton after falling badly from his gig some months earlier.

The firm now known as Wilkinsons was founded by one JE Hall and Dr AG Wilkinson's son Oliver. The original business was both carpentry and funeral work.

Today coffins come as a shell which the undertaker lines and applies 'furniture' handles and a plate; back then however coffin-making tools such as saws, hammers, and chisels were used to produce handmade coffins in solid elm and oak, the family often working late into the night to complete and put a final polish to their commissions. Only in much later years would a circular saw be acquired.

In those early days refrigeration was unknown; the firm used dry ice to preserve bodies until the

Above: *Oliver Wilkinson dressed in his funeral attire in the early 1900s. He is pictured carrying Dr A G Wilkinson's (his fathers) bag.*

firm acquired garage premises opposite, at 80 Somerset Street, in 1962 and in 1968 acquired 28 Grove Road as space for a mortuary, chapel and offices.

Since the death of Ray Wilkinson in 1980, and of Thomas Jones in 1989, Nigel Jones remains in sole charge, priding himself in carrying out full funeral requirements in a traditional and dignified manner, much the same today as carried out by two generations of his family before him.

funeral. All members of the family were expected to help out: The youngest members of the family were paid a few pennies to hold the horses heads whilst the funeral took place in the church.

In 1921 on the death of Oliver Wilkinson the business was run by his widow Sarah Elizabeth Wilkinson and her son, the firm's embalmer, Raymond Oliver Wilkinson. Ray is still remembered by many of the local senior citizens and ran Wilkinson's for many years with the help of his nephew and great nephew Thomas Oliver Jones and Nigel Oliver Jones. Raymond was a chief inspector of the special constabulary and drove the Mayor in the Northampton carnival because he owned a car.

Originally the firm's horses were stabled at Grove Road whilst motor vehicles, acquired much later, were for some time garaged in Broad Street. The

Until recently the family lived on the premises but, following complete renovations to the property in the mid 1990s that long tradition came to an end. But other traditions such as quality of service survive unimpaired. The world may have changed considerably since Oliver Wilkinson founded the firm in 1877 but the concept of dedicated professionalism has not changed with the passing years.

Today Nigel Jones can still offer a professional service every bit as dignified as that offered by his Victorian relative.

Top left: *The firm's premises.* ***Left:*** *The Funeral Parlour's shattered window following the terrorist bomb blast in 1974.* ***Below:*** *Nigel Jones leading a funeral cortege in modern attire.*

Tinker, tailor.... solicitor!

There can be few Northampton families or businesses which have not at some time in their own histories had dealings with local solicitors Dennis Faulkner & Alsop.

William Dennis, a Northampton man, born in 1816 and admitted as a Solicitor in 1838 was the firm's founder. He commenced practice on his own account in 1838 at an address in Horsemarket and subsequently in Sheep Street. In 1876 he was joined in partnership by Dr John Faulkner, a Doctor of Law who had previously practised in London.

Mr Dennis held a number of legal appointments. He was Perpetual Commissioner for Northamptonshire; Assistant Clerk to the County Council; Registrar of the County Court and District Registrar of the High Court. In addition, he was Alderman and twice Mayor of Northampton. He died in 1882.

When Dr Faulkner joined the partnership the name of the firm became Dennis and Faulkner. Dr Faulkner was also a Registrar of the County Court and District Registrar of the High Court. In 1906 the firm moved from Sheep Street to 17 Market Square. Dr Faulkner died in 1910 but before then one of his sons, Bertram Faulkner, had joined his father in partnership after being admitted as a Solicitor in 1906. The firm became known as Dennis and Faulkners. Bertram Faulkner went on to become President of the Northamptonshire Law Society.

Just prior to Dr Faulkner's death a new Partner, Charles Alsop had arrived. Like Bertram, he too had been articled to the elder Faulkner. The practice became known as Dennis Faulkner and Alsop, the name by which it is still known. Charles Alsop remained with the firm until 1934 when he retired to spend more time working as a Magistrate, eventually becoming Chairman of the Bench before his death in 1953.

In 1922 George Edward Foster joined the partnership. By that time the Partners had purchased another practice, in Daventry. George Foster became Daventry's part time Town Clerk and ran the firm's Daventry office. He retired as Town Clerk in 1945 but remained a Partner until his retirement in 1966. He too became President of the Northamptonshire Law Society.

Bernard Clare Tippleston had been articled to Charles Alsop and joined the partnership in 1934. He succeeded George Foster as Senior Partner in 1967. Bernard Tippleston retired in 1975 and died the same year. He had been a Borough Councillor for a number of years and for part of that time was Chairman of the Housing Committee. He had also been Chairman of the East Midlands Legal Aid Committee and President of the Northamptonshire Law Society.

In 1949 Arthur Leonard Singlehurst became a

Left: William Dennis, founder of the firm in 1838, Dr John Faulkner who joined him in 1876 and Charles Frederick Alsop who became a Partner in 1910.

Partner, having been articled to Bertram Faulkner. In that same year the firm moved to its current address at 32 Market Square. Leonard Singlehurst briefly succeeded Bernard Tippleston as Senior Partner in 1975 before retiring later that year. He died in 1983 having been President of the Northamptonshire Law Society and much involved in local charities such as the Northampton and County Blind Association and the Roadmender Club.

Bernard Tippleston's son Geoffrey Drake Tippleston having been articled in London became a Partner in 1962 but tragically died in 1970 at the early age of 32.

Archibald Geoffrey Gee, who is married to George Foster's daughter, joined the firm in 1954 and became a Partner in 1957. He became Senior Partner in 1975 and retired in 1988. He too was a President of the Northamptonshire Law Society and in addition was President of the Chamber of Commerce and Industry; Chairman of the Social Security Appeal Tribunals; and Chairman of the East Midlands Rent Assessment Committee and Rent Tribunal.

Murray Alexander Lillie Holmes, who was educated at the same school as Geoffrey Tippleston and who was also articled in London, joined the firm in 1966. He became a Partner in 1968 and by a strange coincidence subsequently purchased George Foster's former house in Kingsthorpe. He became Senior Partner in 1989 in succession to Geoffrey Gee. Like his predecessors he too has been President of the Northamptonshire Law Society and he was also Chairman of the Northamptonshire Family Health Services Disciplinary Committee. He is Chairman of two local Charities and a Director of Northampton Saints Plc, the company which owns Northampton Saints Rugby Football Club. He is a former President of that Club.

The Daventry office was sold in 1990. A new "DF&A" office dealing exclusively with commercial legal business was opened in 1996 in Northampton's Cheyne Walk.

Above: *The firm's current premises, Beethoven House to the left of the montage and the Cheyne Walk premises to the right.* ***Right:*** *Mr M A L Holmes, current Senior Partner.*

Quality with quantity

The firm of Ernest Howard was established as a Quantity Surveying practice in Northampton in 1923. Over the years it has changed its name to Ernest Howard & Son and then Howard Associates and now embraces all the most up-to-date techniques in providing its Quantity Surveying, Project Management and Construction Management services.

Ernest Howard founded the original firm in 1923, having previously been a Quantity Surveyor working for a local builder. He practiced as a sole practitioner, working from offices above Watts & Sons, the furnishers in Abington Street, Northampton.

It is universally recognised that there is seldom a good time to start a business, but the 1920s were probably amongst the worst for setting up a Quantity Surveying practice. The post first world war economic situation had yet to turn really sour in 1923 and no doubt Ernest Howard believed that times could only get better. Hard times would however lie ahead. From 1929 until the outbreak of the second world war in 1939, the British economy was in a perilous state and few could have predicted then whether or not the fledgling firm of Ernest Howard would survive.

Despite the hardships of the 1930s, Ernest's son, EJ Howard, came to work with his father. During the second world war however, the firm's founder was left on his own again whilst his son served in the Leicestershire Yeomanry, winning the Croix de Guerre and the Military Cross. In 1945, at the age of 28, Jack re-joined the firm after the second world war and the practice was re-christened Ernest Howard & Son.

Top left: *Company founder Ernest Howard.*
Above right: *Ernest Howard's son, Ernest 'Jack' Howard. When he joined the practice it became Ernest Howard & Son.* **Right:** *The Express Lift Tower, Northampton.*

During the 1950s the firm moved to offices in Derngate, over the old bus station, and in 1967 it moved to its present location at 67 The Avenue, Cliftonville.

During the 1960s both of Jack's sons, George and Jonathan, joined the firm, having both qualified a Quantity Surveyors at the College of Estate Management in London. They brought with them new ideas and, together with their partners, John Smith and Paul Butcher, they pioneered the management techniques of Project Management and Construction Management, for which the company is best known today.

During the 1970s and 1980s the firm continued to expand and in 1987 the firm was

High School for Girls, Northampton Boys' school and the Carlsberg Brewery. In addition, they were involved with many of the colleges and pubs, the extensions to the Town Hall, and the present Chronicle & Echo building.

In recent years their Construction Management commissions have taken the company to all parts of the United Kingdom and they have recently completed projects for Computacenter at Hatfield; DHL at East Midlands Airport; Iceland at Enfield; Booker in Edinburgh; and IKEA at Bristol.

During the last 78 years, the business founded by Ernest Howard has grown from being a one-man operation to an enterprise that is involved in building projects costing millions of pounds throughout the whole of the UK. Who could have foreseen, back in 1923 that a small business that began above a furniture shop in Abington Street would one day become the major undertaking that it is today?

incorporated and changed its name to become Ernest Howard Ltd, trading as Howard Associates. In 1988 the company became part of the Fletcher King Group Plc, a move which gave it a greater public profile and enabled it to establish offices in London, Birmingham and Manchester, as well as its Northampton base.

During the firm's life, few major buildings in Northampton have not felt the benefit of Howard's expertise: they acted as Quantity Surveyors on many of the town's housing estates and high rise blocks of flats and, as Project Managers, they oversaw the construction of the Express Lift Tower, St Benedict's Church, the

Top left: *An aerial view of Northampton with the Carlsberg Tetley brewery in the foreground.*
Above left: *Northampton Town Hall.*
Right: *The firm's board of directors, from left to right, standing; Jonathan Mepham, Terry Harding, John Smith and Jonathan Howard. From left to right seated; George Howard, Paul Butcher and Donald Loe.*

Helping Northampton businesses succeed

With a track record of providing professional accounting services to the businesses of Northampton which extends back over forty years, Dove Naish are on their way to achieving their ambition of becoming the preferred choice for all local businesses. They presently have offices in two other locations in the county, Daventry and Towcester, but the first office was in the centre of Northampton when the roots of the present firm started in 1960.

The founding partner, Jack Dove, commenced articles in September, 1950. He entered into an informal partnership agreement with Alfred Smith in 1960 and worked from rented rooms in Eastgate House, 11 Cheyne Walk, Northampton, an early 19th century building with a Regency neo-classical facade. In the early 1900s this had been a select school for ladies run by a Miss Elizabeth Bromwich and had subsequently been the private residence of a doctor and later still a residential and commercial hotel. The Eastgate

House property was acquired by the practice by sealed tender and this was partly funded by a sale of the rear of the premises. Inevitably this led to a restriction of development potential.

Jack Dove built up his share of the partnership through the acquisition of other accountancy firms, and in this way gained quality clients who were well-connected. His own hard work and commitment brought new business and his client base soon trebled in size. Andrew Naish joined the firm in 1965. The firm became known as Smith, Dove and Partners.

By the early 1970s the firm had established offices in Daventry, Towcester and Wellingborough and Richard Parkinson who had entered into articles with the firm in 1965 became a partner in 1973. It was a time of great change, even upheaval, in the make-up of the firm's personnel.

Below: *Eastgate House in the late 1800s.*

There was continual commitment in these early years to educate staff and clients. The introduction of VAT in 1973 brought a significant opportunity to communicate with clients and a successful seminar was held to introduce this completely new concept in taxation. This was followed by others on different topics. A standards committee was also brought into being.

The practice has always been fortunate in having excellent staff throughout its history and has benefited from their efficiency, skills and loyalty. Several current members of staff joined the firm in the 1960s. To improve recruitment and work satisfaction a social committee was formed and various events took place. A football team (with occasional guests) played 'friendly' games and then entered the Northampton Sunday League with some success.

> *The practice has always benefited from the efficiency, skills and loyalty of it's staff*

The business expanded steadily from the early days at Eastgate House and 70 Derngate was acquired as an annexe. Car parking was a permanent problem and on one occasion Andrew Naish arranged for the purchase of a chain and the car of an unauthorised visitor was duly padlocked to the dustbin!

The 1970s were a period of rapid growth and gradually more office and archive space became necessary and another move became imperative. After a long search Eagle House at 28 Billing Road was found and acquired by tender from Northamptonshire County Council for £111,111. The Northampton base of the firm is there to this day.

Andrew Naish considered the occasion of the move to new premises to be a good one to retire

Above: *Eagle House, now home to Dove Naish.*

from practice and left in May 1982 to pursue his love of steam locomotives. The transfer to Billing Road was successfully undertaken in two moves and construction work added an extension to the Victorian building together with increased car park capacity.

Jack Dove retired in 1992 but remains a respected member of the local community.

There are seven partners at present: John Henderson, Head of Human Resources, who is a keen golfer, considering himself now too old for rugby, cricket, squash and football. John has been both Treasurer and Captain of Kingsthorpe Golf Club; Zinaida Silins, Head of the Small Business Unit throughout the practice; Ian Robson, Head of Financial Services and responsible for running the Towcester Office; Peter Merriman, Managing Partner, whose family has been in Northampton for as long as anyone can remember - his father was a Chartered Accountant and company secretary for United Counties for most of his working life, his brother is a District Judge; Russell Wright, Commercial Partner and Head of Client Services with responsibility for Dove Naish computer network systems; Richard Parkinson, Finance Partner, whose family has been in Northampton for four generations, his great-grandfather, grandfather and father successively ran Abel & Sons, the music business on Market Square (originally founded in 1794, but closed in 1970 to make way for the Grosvenor Centre), he is a member of Nene Valley Rotary Club which he has served in the office of both President and Treasurer and drove an aid lorry out to Romania on their behalf, he is also a keen sailor and finally Vaughan Griffiths, Head of the Audit

Team, who has had extensive involvement in charitable work through his connections with the United Reform Church and various other charities in the town, his mother ran Carnival Wallpaper (now Carnival Taylor), he is a qualified BCF coach as well as being President of Northamptonshire Schools Chess Association, he also is a keen musician playing the cello.

The partners have always been concerned to maximise efficiency and computer technology was introduced in the early years 1980s. Upgrading of equipment has been a constant feature ever since giving all members of the firm fluency in IT matters.

Dove Naish have an enviable reputation for providing practical advice and a complete accountancy service for their clients. They are large enough to cope with the demands of large companies, yet small enough to care for the sole trader or medium-sized operation.

Today Dove Naish offers a complete range of accountancy services, including tax planning and management, accounting systems, audit, accounts preparation, VAT support, company secretarial advice as well as IT advice. They also provide payroll and accounts and administration services for clients who do not have their own in-house accounts teams and prefer to outsource these services. The firm offers advice on financial planning for individuals and companies, including strategic planning for business development and succession.

Above: *The firm's current partners outside Eagle House from left to right Russell Wright, Zinaida Silins, Peter Merriman, Vaughan Griffiths, Johm Henderson, Richard Parkinson and Ian Robson.*

Engineering their own fine reputation

The extensive experience gained working in local Northampton engineering companies gave Edward (Ted) Robinson the confidence to branch out on his own and set up the Crane Hill Engineering Company in 1963. That company is now still going strong and the tradition of providing customers with quality work backed up by a reputation for reliability which was so firmly established by Ted is now, forty years later, being continued by his three sons, Geoff, Michael and Robert.

Ted set up his first workshop at 68-70 Grafton Street, Northampton in premises owned by H C Wilcox whose business involved doing chassis welding for MOT repairs. This area became known as Crane Hill because in the 40s and 50s cranes would regularly struggle to negotiate the hill and this is how the fledgling firm got its name. Crane Hill Engineering's workshop space consisted of a small lean-to and their original 'capital equipment' included an old five gallon oil drum in which holes had been drilled - this was supplied with coke and served as the infant firm's source of heating.

In the early days of the business, Edward worked from six in the morning to six in the evening when he would take the days production home for his wife, Mary to swage on a small press on the kitchen table. These inserts were then used to strengthen the heels of stilletto heeled shoes made by a firm in Bedfordshire. Following his tea Edward would then return to work until around midnight. He would be up again by four o'clock to deliver the inserts to Bedford. This went on for

nearly a year until they started to do work for Bostroms.

In common with many setting out in business, the Robinsons had their difficulties to overcome. For Ted these came in the shape of the credit squeeze in 1966. To ensure the continued viability of his company, Ted worked at his business during the day and drove a lorry at night. Geoff, one of his sons had to be laid off at this time.

In the mid-1960s a fruitful working partnership was formed which remains to this day. Crane Hill started doing work for a company called UOP Bostrom, which now trades as Kab Seating, part of the Bostrom Group of companies.

A mark of the success enjoyed by the firm in its first ten years or so of trading is that their original premises became too small for their requirements and so, in 1975, they moved a few doors down the street to the engineers' workshop at the rear of the old chrome tanning premises on the corner of Grafton Street and St Andrew's Road. The workshop entrance was in Francis Street. But continued growth soon meant they outgrew this work space as well and two years later the company moved to rented premises in Mill Lane, Semilong.

While concentrating his outlay on equipment which ensured he did the best possible job for his clients, Ted made do with more Spartan arrangements as far as his personal comfort was

Above: *Edward 'Ted' Robinson, founder of the firm.*

concerned. There was no room for a separate area for tea and meal breaks, so Ted made extensive use of the facilities offered by The Four Fishes Café in St Andrew's Road. At The Spotted Dog public house he played and ran a skittle team with the menfolk there. This was an ideal way to relax and helped Ted take his mind off the pressures of his business. This was a spot favoured by a number of Northampton's 'characters' - and many jokes were shared and numerous anecdotes told.

Over the intervening years, all the Robinson sons came into the business and contributed to its ongoing success and allowing it to expand and diversify its operations. One upshot of this was that the firm found itself once more in need of increased workshop space and so in 1987 they were on the move once again. This time it was to premises they were able to buy themselves. These premises, located in Harvey Reeves Road, St. James, Northampton, have served the company well since that time.

The move provided the impetus for further expansion and diversification, and father and sons were joined by Lionel Parker, an old family friend, who brought his knowledge and expertise of line boring, head testing and axle repairs to the company. The company was reorganised into Production Shop and Engine Shop sections, the Engine shop undertaking commercial engine plant repairs. Machining of repaired ship heads was an important part of their operations at this time. The firm acquired more and more specialist equipment and now has a comprehensive range of workshop equipment including lathes and presses, drilling machines, millers in the Production workshop and union borers, cylinder head pressure equipment, machines for carrying out axle repairs, cylinder head grinders and specialised welding equipment in the Engine Shop.

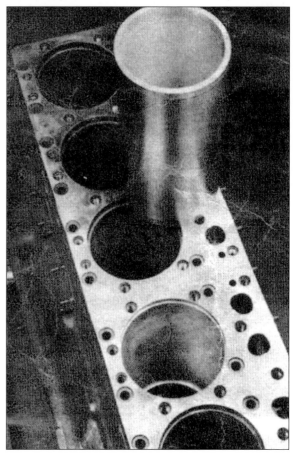

Ted had the satisfaction of seeing the fruit of his hard work in the establishing of the business as a well respected company in its field, operating from its own premises and providing high quality service to its clients. It was a sad day for all connected with the firm when he died in June 1991.

The traditions of good service and quality work has since that time been continued by his sons. The eldest, Geoff runs the production side of things and Michael and Robert see to the operation of the Engine Shop.

Top right: *Inserting top counter bores.*
Above: *Re-sleeving cracked bores.*

The company was pleased to be awarded BS5750 status, a mark of the quality of their work in 1995. This achievement was followed three years later by accreditation to the prestigious and sought after ISO 9000 standard.

Crane Hill Engineering, while having much in which it can take pride in its history is nevertheless a forward-looking concern and is pleased to embrace new technology and methods where they can contribute to the development of the business in a way which help them meet the requirements of their clients. The start of the new century saw them launch their own web-site and friends and customers alike may learn about what the company has to offer by visiting www.cranehilleng.com. While this is certainly a

useful means of giving information, it is unlikely that it will replace the personal telephone and face-to-face contact which has always been a hallmark of the Crane Hill way of going about things, a method which has ensured that the customer has been supplied with work of the highest quality.

Crane Hill expertise, built up over the last forty years is available to all customers, together with an approach which takes the view that 'anything's possible' - this attitude was the basis of Ted's commercial vision in the 1960s and will be continued by the firm in the future.

*Left: An engine block being put on a boring machine for line boring by Ted. **Below:** Lionel Parker with brothers, Mick, Rob and Geoff Robinson alongside one of the firm's vehicles.*

Striking the right note

One of the Northampton area's longest established business is that of Pianoforte Supplies Ltd based at the Simplex Works in Roade. No doubt to the surprise of strangers to the area, despite its name, the firm does not in fact manufacture pianos.

Founded in London, in March 1919, by Cyril Cripps (later Sir Cyril) the company did however originally produce component parts from brass and steel for pianos such as pedals, castors, lifter bars, candle holders, strings and hinges.

Prior to establishing his own firm the founder had worked for Musical Components Ltd, a firm based in Camberwell, where he had been in charge of buying, sales, costings, and wages. There is no doubt that setting up in business to manufacture parts for pianos was a solid investment at that time. There was a short-lived economic boom, affluence seemed to be spreading and the acquisition of a piano was still the dream of many. Many readers will look back with nostalgia to the days of their childhood and recall just how common it once was to enter a house and discover an upright piano leaning against the wall of a

Above: *Company founder Sir Cyril Cripps.*
Below: *The old smithy where the fledgling firm began life in 1919.*

front room or parlour, sometimes played but as often as not a silent testimony to thrift and hard work and serving as both a plant stand and status symbol. Who could have predicted back in 1919 that the wireless and record players, let alone music centres and CDs, would one day provide us all with as much, and often much more, music in our homes than we need and would gradually supplant the once loved piano in much of the public's affections.

But tape decks and Radio One were still far in the future in 1919, and a world weary of four years of war was eager to get round their pianos once more and play happier tunes and sing more joyful songs than had been possible for some time.

The new firm's first premises were at Saville Place, Lambeth. It subsequently moved to the larger premises of the old Simplex Shoe Polish factory at Roade in January 1923. From the original small firm with just seven employees the business would steadily expand and diversify to manufacture metal components for many industries including the automobile, aircraft, piano and cabinet trades.

Despite a near disastrous fire in November 1933 by the outbreak of war in 1939 Pianoforte Supplies Ltd employed 350 people and had customers all over the country with regular deliveries to London, Coventry, Oxford, Birmingham and Luton.

During the second world war the piano and motor trade work halted and nearly all production was for the war effort. Munitions, aircraft parts, steel helmets, smoke floats, flame floats and pyrotechnic containers were made. One important item was a parachute flare which was to save the lives of many Allied airmen of the pathfinder squadrons during night bombing raids. Previously flares dropped to light the target areas also silhouetted the aircraft against the night sky making them easy targets for anti-aircraft guns. The company manufactured a modified flare with a parachute shaped metal reflector which gave cover to the aircraft by reflecting the intense light downwards. The development of the parachute flare led to the firm's founder being awarded the MBE at the war's close. One can only wonder if any of those

Above: *The old Simplex Shoe Polish factory at Roade.*

brave RAF crewmen ever made the connection between the parachute flares they used and the pub piano they stood round, singing and drinking in celebration of a successful mission.

After the war the company reverted to its normal peacetime projects, the greater part of the output now being for the automobile industry. In 1948 in the post war economic recovery turnover quadrupled requiring 200 extra employees. By 1952 over 800 people were employed requiring special buses to bring them from Northampton and from neighbouring villages.

> *By 1952 over 800 people were employed requiring special buses to bring them to work*

Throughout the 1950s demand for cars increased dramatically and by the end of 1959 (the year of the mini car) the workforce topped 1,700. The factory expanded: new buildings were erected to house an enlarged toolroom, press shop and light engineering shop with further polishing, plating and packing facilities. Production was now geared to manufacturing chrome plated trims such as radiator grills, hub caps and body side mouldings, mild steel door frames and various rolled steel sections for the cars of the period - although hinges and piano strings were still being made. The 1960s saw more steady progress and by 1969 the workforce peaked at over 1,800.

In the seventies car design moved away from chrome to painted metal or plastic trim and this, together with a greater degree of automation and a recession, led to the workforce falling back to 700 by 1980. Piano string manufacture had ceased in 1979.

In 1979 however the company had acquired a small manufacturing business at Wellesbourne, Warwickshire producing plastic to metal co-extrusions and rubber to metal bonded bearings. New co-extrusion lines were also installed at the Roade factory and the workforce learned the art of producing plastic/metal co-extrusions and the decorative plastic/metal assemblies now required by car manufacturers.

Today Pianoforte Supplies Ltd employs over 400 people at Roade and some 150 at Wellesbourne. Car components are still the main items and are sold to all major motor manufacturers. Products are manufactured from rolled sections, pressings, metal and plastic co-extrusions, plastic injection mouldings and rubber to metal bonded bearings. Items may be anodised, plated or powder coated. And, in a reminder of the firm's origins, continuous 'piano' hinges are still produced.

In many ways Pianoforte Supplies is a unique firm, perhaps one of its most significant attributes is the loyalty of its workforce: in the many decades since the firm moved to Roade over 700 employees have completed more than 25 years continuous service with the firm whilst over 20 employees have managed to clock up 50 years of continuous service.

And four generations of the Cripps family have been associated with the firm. Prominent amongst them the founder's son, Humphrey Cripps, was made Deputy Lieutenant of Northamptonshire in 1986 after being made High Sheriff of Northampton in 1985; he received a knighthood from the Queen in 1989.

From piano parts through parachutes to plastics the history of Pianoforte Supplies has been one of continuity judiciously seasoned with change.

Below: *The founders son, the late Sir Humphrey C Cripps.*

A burning ambition

A stranger today visiting the showrooms and works of A Bell & Company in Kingsthorpe Road, Kingsthorpe and seeing the state-of-the-art kitchens, bathrooms, heating appliances and fireplaces on display could be forgiven for thinking that the company arrived in Northampton only yesterday. But nothing could be further from the truth.

It was back in 1898 that the Northampton Mercury carried an advert announcing the opening of Ablett Bell's new ironmongers shop in Gold Street.

Two years later Ablett was joined by the brothers Frank and Harry Jelley to form the two-family partnership which survives to this day. As well as ironmongery the partnership would soon sell kitchen ranges, a new type of open fire and a barless kitchen

range. The Bell Range and Foundry Company's famous Canopy Dog Grates are still made today.

By 1905 the firm had expanded into a four storey warehouse in Kingswell Street in addition to the Gold Street premises. In 1908 the firm became a limited company acquiring its present name; that same year it was to achieve international recognition gaining four gold medals and the Grand Prix for its grates at the Franco English exhibition. Around this time tile interiors and kerbs began to be produced at Kingswell Street, as well as the tiled surrounds which marked the beginning of the fireplace we know today.

*Above: Company founder Mr Ablett Bell. **Right:** Mr Bell's premises in the early 1900s. **Below:** The showroom and offices on Gold Street, 1909.*

From the early days the company's commercial travellers were an important source of business. Local calls would be made by bicycle, whilst visits to far flung places, such as Rugby and Wolverton, would require the traveller to take his cycle on the train. As for deliveries, local orders were taken by horse drawn transport and hand carts whilst out of town orders were delivered by carrier carts based at local taverns and carrying passengers as well as goods.

Bell's first catalogue included a huge number of items: Bell's own cooking ranges and fires, gas lighting, coal-fired coppers, boilers and heating stoves, WCs, wash basins and baths, cisterns, stable stalls and harness room fittings along with a large section of ironmongery. The range continued to expand well into the 1930s to include guttering, pipes, manhole covers as well as plumbing supplies and tools for plumbers, carpenters and bricklayers.

Early heating appliances were mostly designed for solid fuel which called for a very flexible method of installation: a tinsmith made special fittings for each individual job. Heating stoves also became very popular and one of the best remembered is the Heat Storage Esse Cooker used in houses, hotels and hospitals whilst another long remembered item is the Combination Grate which had an open fire combined with one or two ovens and sometimes a fire back boiler.

Engraving plates for coffins was another area of business, they were supplied to country builders who

*Top: The factory premises at Kingsthorpe, built in 1926. **Above right:** A police officer at the scene of devastation following the Stirling Bomber crash in 1941.*

sometimes doubled up as undertakers. Details of the required inscription would be telephoned in and, after engraving, the brass plate would be sent on the bus to its recipient, parceled up with a lining shroud and wadding.

By 1927, the year of Ablett Bell's death, the firm had seen remarkable expansion: By 1923, for example, the firm had opened a London showroom whilst a new production site had to be built to provide purpose built facilities on a three acre site on the Thornton Estate at Kingsthorpe.

The outbreak of war in 1939 saw many changes. A Bell & Co felt the impact of war quite literally when in July 1941 a Stirling bomber crashed on top of the Gold Street premises. The shop front and a great deal of stock were destroyed, whilst two people on firewatch duty had a

narrow escape. It took until September to clear the shop area of debris.

The firm's prestigious London showroom was in Berners Street. Luftwaffe bombing destroyed those premises which were never to reopen. Elsewhere the company's factory at Kingsthorpe had been requisitioned by the War Office; normal production was switched to the making of pre-cast concrete air raid shelters and paraffin lamps. By 1943 all the factory space was being used as stores for the US Army. The iron railings which had once surrounded the factory were removed as salvage to help the war effort and were replaced by ornate concrete wall capping, some of which can still be seen today.

Following the war's end Bell's range of products increased still further to include cutlery, pewter and silverware, vases, fenders, trays, and mirrors, all displayed alongside hardware in Gold Street, with fireplaces and bathroom suites still displayed at Kingswell Street. More space was soon needed.

An answer to the shortage of space came when the old Majestic Cinema in Gold Street was bought and rebuilt so that both showrooms could be housed together. The move was made in 1952 with warehouse goods being transferred to Horseshoe Street opposite.

In 1956 Bell's became a Calor Gas dealer, an appointment which would lead, in future years, to the firm becoming the major supplier of Calor Gas and equipment in Northamptonshire.

The increasing popularity of central heating in the 1970s would lead to a rapid decline in the demand for fireplaces. In recent years, however, a resurgence of interest in open fires has meant that once again fireplaces are in demand with no-one better placed to supply original designs than A Bell & Co.

Since the early 1980s the company has also been a distributor for the famed Aga cooker, originally available for use with solid fuel. Today's models run on oil and gas, ensuring that whatever its location every household can enjoy the benefits of an Aga.

In 1984 the last link with Gold Street was severed when the whole business was moved onto the site at Kingsthorpe Road. The redeveloped premises feature a massive showroom of some 13,000 sq. ft. displaying a wide range of quality products for the home. In this showroom you will now find the leading Kitchen Design Studio in the area, a vast range of Bathroom equipment, and an outstanding Tile Centre alongside one of the largest displays of Fireplaces and heating appliances in the country. Adjoining the main showroom is a Specialist Calor Gas Centre where expert advice is available on the purchase or hire of heating, commercial, catering and outdoor leisure products such as barbecues.

Today with its extensive premises, huge range of craftsman-built products and ample car parking Bell's offers visitors the kind of welcome which Ablett Bell would have been proud of. Displaying the same professionalism, innovation and attention to detail that characterised Bell's in its early years the company is now carrying forward Ablett's remarkable legacy into the 21st century.

Top left: *An Aga cooker circa 1935.*
Below: *The firm's current premises on Kingsthorpe Road, Northampton.*

Bidding for quality

If you have ever been to an auction in Northampton, or have had something to be auctioned, the chances are that you have been in contact with Merry's. Merry's have been putting Northampton's livestock and household chattels under the hammer for nearly two centuries now and are a well established part of Northampton life. The firm started out life in 1815 when a Mr Macquire started in business that year selling stocks and shares by auction, he subsequently extended this work to include the auctioning of livestock, chattels and landed property.

In the 1880s a Mr Tarry joined the practice, also holding the title of Manager of Northampton Opera House in 1884. In 1888, he conducted what was then Northampton's largest auction sale, when he put all properties owned by John Campbell Franklin under the hammer, including the theatre of which he was the manager. A unique dual role! In those days the firm was located opposite the Town Hall at the top of Guildhall Road.

Thomas Merry first appeared in the late 1880s when the firm was then called Mcquire Tarry and Merry. In 1898, the partnership was dissolved and then became known as Macquire and Merry. In 1911, the firm's title changed to Merry & Co and by 1928 the second generation Merrys, Mr J B Merry, better known as Chubb Merry and Mr Norton Merry had joined the practice, then named Merry, Sons and Co Ltd. Chubb Merry died in 1968 and was the last member of the Merry

family to practice as an auctioneer, though family members still live locally. Dick Cowling joined the firm in 1944 as a pupil of Norton Merry which by 1968 had become known as Merry Sons and Cowling. Around this time the firm operated from Fish Street, moving by 1970 to Bridge Street. The equally old established firm of Pierce Thorpe and Marriott was amalgamated into the practice in 1980. The firm has witnessed great changes in the way

Below: *A flat-capped, gavel wielding, Norton Merry at the Northampton Ram Fair in the 1930s.*

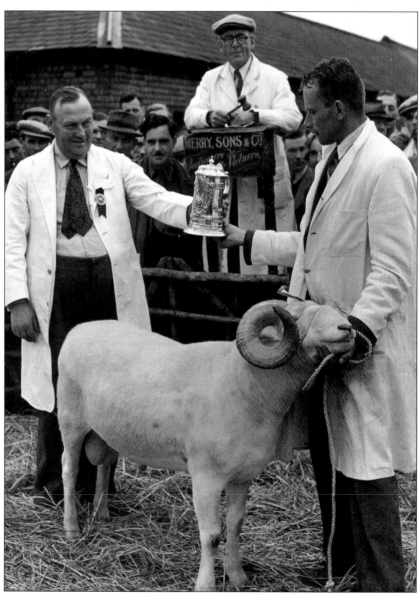

son, Andrew Cowling in 1976. Andrew became the sole proprietor in 1991.

From 1996 the firm has expanded rapidly and their work has been divided between its two divisions, Merry's Residential and Financial Services and Merry's Commercial Ltd. That year also saw the formation of Northamptonshire Auctions PLC with the purpose of building and operating the new Livestock Market at Brackmills. The company raised the necessary £1.3 million capital to develop the new Auction Centre, which includes two purpose built Salerooms. It opened in December 1996. The saleroom is managed by Denise Cowling who since 1992 had been in charge of Merry's auctions at the Old Corn Exchange, Cattlemarket, Victoria Promenade in the town centre.

business is carried out. In the old days goods were moved around by horse and cart when the pace of life was much slower than today. The administrative duties were undertaken by clerks using pen and ink. Nowadays the company makes use of the latest in computer technology to ensure that maximum efficiency is achieved.

The years during and after the Second World war were difficult ones for Merry's as the normal operation of the cattle markets was suspended. Those who lived through those times know only too well that meat was rationed and all livestock was effectively purchased by the Government.

Dick Cowling became sole partner in 1966 and was joined by his

In addition to the two salerooms, there is a livestock market, restaurant and bar, offices, ample car parking and land for expansion; the whole site occupies just under 13 acres in total. Regular sales of Fine Art, Antiques and quality furniture are held on a quarterly basis with monthly sales of general and chattels. Other monthly sales include Horses and Equestrian items, agricultural machinery and motor vehicles. Speciality sales are held on either a half yearly or annual basis. Livestock sales are held on four days every week.

The salerooms have proved to be highly successful under the guidance of Denise and have been a growth area of the practice. The improved facilities at the Auction Centre will enable the Company to further expand the services offered to both Vendor and Purchaser alike, as well as improving the quality of the Sales. They are looking forward to their next two hundred years.

Top right: *At the Ram Fair again, with Dick Cowling (centre) notebook in hand in the 1980s.*
Right: *Merry's town centre offices, Bridge Street.*

A moving story

C Butt Ltd is one of the region's best known transport contractors, and the firm's history goes back a long way.

Charles Butt left the forces in 1919 and bought 12 acres of land in Weedon Road which he used for market gardening and pig rearing. Having a horse and cart he was able to undertake casual haulage work for the council and his fledgling transport business soon prospered.

In 1926 Charles was joined by his nephew William 'Bill' Butt and before long their first tipper lorry was acquired which was soon to replace their horse drawn transport. As the operation grew, larger additional vehicles and a property at Stenson Street were acquired. Regular runs were being made to London, Liverpool and Bristol for local mills, contractors, builders and breweries. Often

Top left: WH Butt (the Guv'nor) a founder of the company. Right: The first brand new diesel engined vehicle purchased by Butts; a 1947 ERF 54G. Below: 1959 Scammell Highwayman 25 tons low loader.

return loads were off-loaded at Stenson Street and vehicles reloaded for the next day. Local work continued to be important: deliveries for allotment holders and stall holders at Northampton market were made as well as carrying sand and gravel from local sandpits.

With the increase in scale the Weedon Road Garage was acquired where the maintenance of the vehicles took place and Cyril Starr was recruited in 1946.

During the second word war some of the vehicles had to be allocated to work for the Ministry of War, and a percentage of lorries had to be converted to run on gas. By the closing year of the war 22 vehicles were being operated.

At least driver shortages would end with the war - despite drivers' wages in 1946 being just 75 shillings (£3 75p) for a 48 hour week with a maximum of 68 hours.

New workshops, offices and a lorry park were erected in Spencer Bridge Road in 1954. The following year C Butt Ltd was created with the original shareholders being Charles Butt, William H Butt and Cyril Starr.

BJ Butt joined C Butt Ltd on completion of National Service in 1956 and was soon working for ST Callis Ltd, a cattle haulage company based in Badby and bought by Butts in 1952.

In the years that followed acquisition would follow acquisition: Ritchie and Hooks Ltd of Liverpool was bought as was Willis Transport of Sutton Coldfield.

Meanwhile Charles Butt still worked on his market gardening with part of the land now used to park some of his lorries.

Manager Tom Crouch died in 1947 and was succeeded by Cyril Starr, his assistant.

In 1948 the Labour Government nationalised road transport and C & WH Butt was taken over by the Road Haulage Executive and came under the control of the British Road Services - in protest at the changes Cyril Starr left the firm.

Cyril Starr joined Bill Butt working at the Weedon Road garage under the name of A Butt, a separate firm operating three tipper lorries and licensed to work only within a 25 mile radius of their base.

Other small local forms were soon bought out by A Butt giving the new business 14 vehicles, each with separate licensing restrictions. An arrangement with Mackay Transport Ltd soon allowed A Butt to recommence long haulage work. Not all work was commercial. In 1953 several tippers had to be allocated for work on sea defence repair caused by the East coast floods. Butt lorries carried slag from Scunthorpe and Immingham to the disaster areas.

More members of the family joined the firm, Gerald Butt in 1960 - now the company Chairman, followed by John Butt, and then by their sons, Robert and Jonathon in the 1980s. Clive Hodgkinson joined the company in 1983 as General Manager.

Butt vehicles continued to haul building materials for many local landmarks: the M1 motorway, the second cooling tower (now gone) at Northampton Power Station and the Express Lift Tower.

Charles Butt, the firm's founder passed away in 1980. By the time Cyril Starr retired in 1983 the company was operating more than 120 vehicles. A remarkable achievement which started with a horse and cart in 1919. In the 1980s and 90s the company continued to expand winning several industry awards and opening depots in Corby, Wellingborough, Middlewich and Wakefield, and is now operating in exess of 200 vehicles.

In 2000 this award winning firm acquired more premises on the Lodge Farm Industrial estate and looks set to make even greater progress.

When de-nationalisation had begun in 1952 Charles and Bill Butt were able to provide the finance needed to buy back a number of vehicles from BRS - all licensed to travel to any part of the United Kingdom.

Top left: The world's first ERF 8 wheeler to be powered by a Cummins diesel engine. First registered in 1962.
Right: ERF EC11 41 tons GTW articulated outfit.

Bathers in their hundreds
enjoying the Midsummer
Meadow Baths during the
hot summer of 1966.

Acknowledgments

*The publishers would like to thank Alan Burman
for providing many of the photographs within this
book, and also for help in the course of research
and proof-reading.*

*Thanks are also due to
Andrew Mitchell who penned the editorial text
and Steve Ainsworth for his copywriting skills*